KRICKET

AN INDIAN-INSPIRED COOKBOOK

'[Kricket is] 100 times better than you would expect ... places like this are the reason why London is the envy of Paris and New York.' – Michel Roux Jr.

I would like to dedicate this book to my grandmother,
Margaret Bell, who inspired me from an early age with her brilliant cooking.
She would have loved Kricket, so this one is for you, Danny x

KRICKET

AN INDIAN-INSPIRED COOKBOOK

by

WILL BOWLBY

Photography by

HUGH JOHNSON

hardie grant books

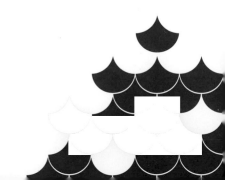

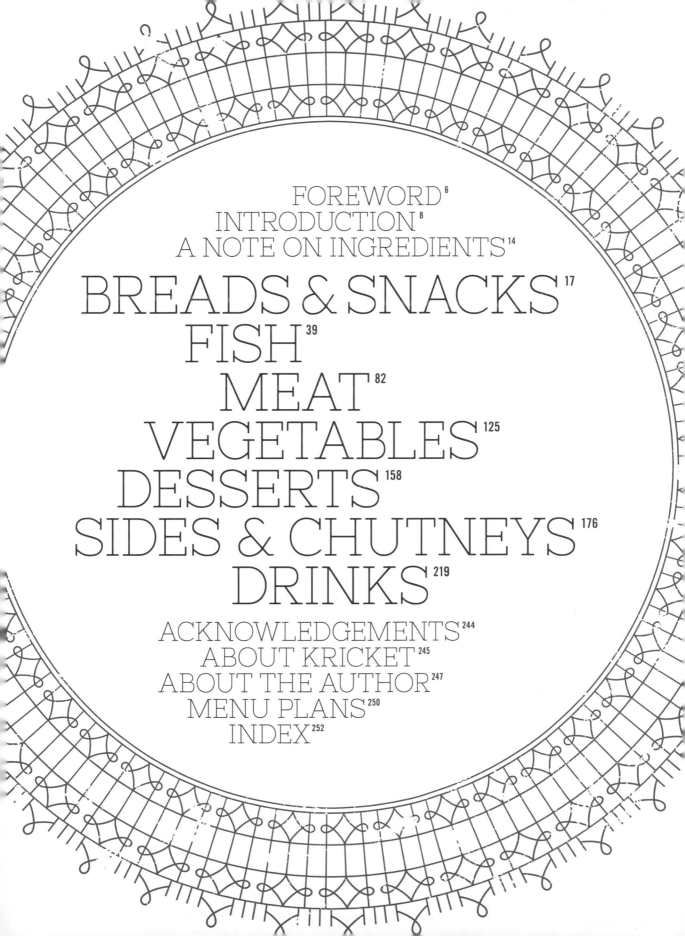

FOREWORD

Because I am French, people think I may have little time for other types of cuisines, but I am excited by all kinds of cooking, flavours and ingredients.

I was surprised when I visited India, a few years ago, at just how much I enjoyed the variety of food and dishes. I'd never tasted curries like these before and I didn't taste that kind of Indian cooking again, until I visited Will's restaurant, Kricket, in London.

Will served me a beautifully spiced, first class vindaloo that transported me back to India – it was delicious. His ability to recognise the importance of balance in food and to let the ingredients do the work, is what makes the food at Kricket so special. Strong flavours, like those typically associated with Indian cooking, require restraint and judgement, and those are the qualities that Will displays in his cooking. His focus is on the quality of the produce itself and everything else is designed to enhance that ingredient's flavour and appeal.

I never expected a young Englishman to show such mastery of Indian cuisine. I haven't asked him to tutor me, but I am hoping to learn a thing or two from this book.

PIERRE KOFFMANN

INTRODUCTION

As far back as I can remember, I have always been passionate about food. My earliest memory is of my mother's chicken in a pot, a herby, unctuous dish that kick-started my five-year-old taste buds and began my love affair with all things to do with food. My maternal grandmother was a huge influence on me; she had lived in post-war East Africa for over a quarter of a century and was a terrific cook. She had a number of very close Indian and Goan friends and had learned skills from them over the years; her curry lunches (for up to 60 people) were legendary, and introduced me – at a very early age – to the delicate layering and spicing of meat and fish.

So I started young, and by the age of ten I was hooked; Jamie Oliver had just come on the scene and he was so inspiring. His can-do approach to food was so cool and made me think: 'yes, that's what I want to do. I want to be a chef!'

While still at school, I set up my own one-man catering company, Will2Cook, providing food for private dinner parties and events, which helped fund my gap year and my time at university. After three wonderful years at Newcastle University, I joined renowned chef Rowley Leigh at his flagship restaurant Le Café Anglais in London. He lived up to his promise to 'throw me in at the deep end'. I started on simple dishes, such as creamed spinach, and over the next two years, worked my way up through all the disciplines, until I was eventually made chef de partie.

I was then approached by a colleague working in India. The owners of Khyber, the oldest and most respected Indian restaurant in Mumbai, were looking for a young English chef to work on the concept of a modern European restaurant they were planning to open in the heart of the city. Following a couple of chaotic trials in London (which gave me a good indication of what was to follow!), I was offered a job in a country I had never visited and knew even less about. On a cold, rainy day in October 2012 I found myself, at the age of 24 with only one business contact, at Heathrow airport boarding a flight to Mumbai to face the biggest challenge of my life so far.

For nearly two years I lived alone in a flat in south Mumbai. I was responsible for a kitchen staff of 20, many of whom spoke no English. The dishes I was asked to create were based on the idea of European recipes that would appeal to the Indian palate. I wasn't to know then that the Indian palate is a many-layered and complicated concept, influenced by religion, ethnicity and cultural preferences. We worked extremely hard as a team, often in challenging and difficult circumstances, and it paid off when we won *The Times of India* award for the Best New European Restaurant. I spent the next few months on the menus at Khyber and, in my spare time, had Indian cooking lessons with the private chef of a famous Mumbai art dealer in his kitchen, who suggested I might one day combine the different techniques I had learned to create a 'fusion restaurant'.

It was here that my fledgling business plan began to take shape. I was so inspired and excited by the different regional cuisines, and started to think about how I could apply my new knowledge that to the fast-food craze taking place in the UK, where I sensed there was a gap in the market between the traditional high street curry house and the high-end expensive Indian restaurants. My research took me to the street stalls of Mumbai where I discovered new favourites: masala dosa – a wafer-thin, crispy Indian pancake filled with potato and spices; and another intensely marinated snack, bright red from its masala sauce. 'What's this?' I asked. 'Goat's nipple,' the vendor told me. Suddenly all sorts of culinary possibilities began to show themselves.

I handed in my notice and embarked on a three-month road trip to see as much of India as I could in my search for the perfect street food. In Goa, I ate super-fresh oysters with coconut cream and chilli in a tiny roof-top restaurant 10 minutes from Arambol beach. In the old city of Delhi, I discovered butter chicken and spicy little kebabs. In Ladakh, where the dusty desert runs into snow-capped mountains of astonishing beauty, the Nepalese momos (small dumplings stuffed with spiced vegetables) were an unexpected delight.

Family connections landed me an invitation to a smart mansion in Lucknow where I downed a glass of a suspiciously green smoothie before being led into the old town's warren of alleyways to a street cart serving sensational shami kebabs: a snack originally created for a toothless Nawab, and made by massaging goat meat and then grinding it down to a paste. Travelling on by train, I ate simple but delicious dal curries, served with rice, chapati and pickles in airline-style trays, made with a pride that would put many restaurants, back home, to shame. The highlights in Calcutta were kathi rolls: chicken and egg wrapped in buttery paratha; and misti doi, a sumptuous pudding of yogurt served with cardamom, rose and pistachio (see my version on page 164).

With time – and money – running out, I returned to England with a head full of ideas and a plan of action: I wanted to explore the idea of taking traditional recipes from the different regions and giving them a twist. Using only the very best of British seasonal ingredients (something I found lacking in India where so much of the highest-quality produce, especially meat and fish, is destined for the export market), I would produce delicious, affordable food showcasing the diversity and intricacy of the recipes to create a contemporary Indian cuisine, presenting it in the new concept of a limited menu offering small plates of food to share. It was an idea that needed working on, and rather than pretending to know how to master the cuisine, I joined top chef Vivek Singh in his flagship restaurant in the City of London, and built on my fledgling knowledge of how to cook with spices. A year later I left, and Kricket was born.

The opportunity to open a restaurant in a 12-metre (40-foot) shipping container in Pop Brixton in South London was presented to me and my business partner, Rik Campbell, in the spring of 2015. Rik and I had met at Newcastle University; his background in events, and his accountancy training, brought necessary and invaluable skills to the business. Rik is front of house and manages all strategic and marketing aspects of Kricket. We built a tiny 20-seater restaurant with a kitchen at one end with our very limited funds and opened in June 2015 with a small menu offering seasonal small plates and Indian-inspired cocktails.

Nothing could have prepared me for the reaction from our customers and the press. Within a year of opening, we had been reviewed by virtually every publication, both online and in print. *The Good Food Guide* included us in their list of the top 25 new restaurants 'representing the very best in an impressively strong field of new entries'; we won the Dot London Small Business Award, were named by *The Sunday Times* as one of the top restaurants for under £20 per head and were shortlisted for

the *Evening Standard's* Restaurant Awards. Over
and above this, the most exciting and humbling
experience, especially for me, were the visits and
generous endorsements from reknowned chefs
such as Pierre Koffmann, Michel Roux Jr and
Nuno Mendes. We also attracted the attention of
the White Rabbit Growth Fund, headed by Chris
Miller, formerly finance director of Soho House.
With their backing, we were able to secure a lease
on a former Italian restaurant on Denman Street in
Soho, London, and in January 2017 we opened a
70-seater restaurant on two floors with an L-shaped
counter opposite an open kitchen on the ground
floor, and tables downstairs for larger parties.
There are plans for other ventures, including a
delivery service, but whatever happens in the
future, I shall remain committed to the original
concept of marrying quality ingredients with the
exhilarating spices of this complex and constantly
evolving cuisine. As a chef, it provides me with
wonderful opportunities to develop, be creative
and to have fun.

I hope whoever reads this book, can understand
that cooking Indian food needn't be a daunting
task. Like any cuisine, once you have learnt the
basics, the possibilities are endless!

WILL BOWLBY

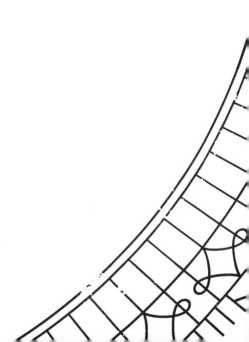

A NOTE ON INGREDIENTS

In the restaurant, I never compromise on the quality of our ingredients. Our meat and fish is sourced locally within the British Isles and never from abroad. With such fantastic quality at our fingertips, we use them carefully and with respect to make sure that with every dish, you can identify and taste the main ingredient, supported by the spices we use rather than letting them mask the flavour of the star ingredient.

STORE CUPBOARD ESSENTIALS:

Every household should have a place for spices and, as long as they are kept in airtight containers, they will keep for longer. Spices can be expensive, so buying them in bulk and storing them properly means that you will save money in the long term and you will always have something to hand when you have that craving for something spicy! I have listed out the store cupboard essentials that will be useful to have in stock when trying out recipes from this book.

BASMATI RICE – always use good-quality basmati rice and you will notice the difference. Make sure you thoroughly rince the rice grains and, ideally, soak them for up to 30 minutes before cooking.

BAY LEAVES – beautifully frangrant, bay leaves add a delicate flavour to rice and most curries. Ideally, always use fresh leaves. They can be stored in an airtight container for a week or two.

BLACK CARDAMOM PODS – expensive and strong in aroma, use sparingly.

CHAAT MASALA – tangy and sightly hot, chaat masala is the perfect seasoning. Only a small pinch is required, but the impact is great. I use it in most of my meat marinades and sprinkle it over fried vegetables for extra zing.

CURRY LEAVES – difficult to get hold of unless you visit specialist Asian stores. Use fresh rather than frozen or dried as the flavour difference is incomparable. Keep in the fridge.

DRIED KASHMIRI RED CHILLIES – the most superior of all chillies, not as hot as some chillies, but they lend a fantastic colour and smoky flavour to tarkas and curries.

GREEN CARDAMOM PODS – beautifully aromatic, crush the pods open after roasting to release the little seeds within the shell.

KASHMIRI RED CHILLI POWDER – bright red in colour and smoky in flavour, it's the only chilli powder we use in the restaurant.

LENTILS AND PULSES – there are a vast number of dried lentils and pulses available in the supermarkets these days. Healthy, versatile and with a long shelf life, they are the perfect store cupboard ingredient.

MUSTARD SEEDS – we use mostly black mustard seeds for the recipes in this book, but there are lots of varieties. Great to use in the base of many south Indian dishes, and good for pickling and preserving.

TURMERIC POWDER – bright yellow in colour and used a lot in Indian cooking, bringing vibrancy and beneficial health properties to the dishes. Be careful not to use too much, it should be seen but not be overpowering.

BREADS & SNACKS

We serve a variety of kulchas (or small naan breads) in our restaurant and they are cooked to order in our tandoor oven. We realise that most of you don't have the luxury of a tandoor in your kitchen, so we have adapted these recipes so they can be made at home. You could treat these breads as flatbreads by cooking them over a medium to high heat on a *tawa* or in a large non-stick frying pan. For best results, though, try recreating a pizza oven by turning on your grill (broiler) to the highest setting, placing a deep, heavy baking pan upside-down underneath the grill and placing your kulchas on that. The refracted heat from the grill onto the pan will cook the dough as fast as possible throughout.

KULCHA DOUGH

Kulcha is a type of leavened bread originating from the Indian subcontinent, especially famous in Amritsar and eaten in India and Pakistan. It can be made from maida flour (wheat flour) but here we use self-raising flour. It is usually eaten with chole (chickpeas), but we serve them in the restaurant with a variety of toppings.

Combine the milk, eggs, sugar, salt, two-thirds of the water and the vegetable oil in a jug or bowl.

Sift the flour into a bowl. Gradually incorporate the wet ingredients into the flour and combine to form a smooth dough, adding a little more water, if necessary, as you knead. Once the dough is smooth, place it on a lightly floured surface, cover it with a damp cloth and leave to rest for about 30 minutes.

Once the dough is rested, divide it into 10 portions of about 80 g (3 oz) each and roll into round balls. Place on a lightly oiled baking sheet, cover as before and set aside until ready to use.

MAKES 10 FLATBREADS

130 ml (4½ fl oz/generous ½ cup) full-fat (whole) milk
4 large free-range eggs
2 tablespoons caster (superfine) sugar
2 teaspoons sea salt
100 ml (3½ fl oz/scant ½ cup) cold water, plus extra if needed
100 ml (3½ fl oz/scant ½ cup) vegetable oil, plus extra for oiling
500 g (1 lb 2 oz/4 cups) self-raising flour, plus extra for dusting

MASALA KULCHA

This bread has been on the menu in our Soho restaurant since day one, and is very popular. It's perfect for vegetarians. Adding a little chaat masala to the finished bread really enhances the whole flavour, so much so that it can be devoured simply with a light brushing of butter. The next few pages showcase other exciting ways you can eat this delicous bread.

Add a generous pinch of coriander and onion to each dough ball and roll to incorporate in the dough, then roll out into 15 cm (6 in) circles on a lightly floured surface.

Place the flatbreads, one at a time, on a hot, dry *tawa* or in a large frying pan (skillet) and cook for 3–4 minutes on each side until puffed up, lightly browned and charred in places.

Remove from the pan, brush the bread generously with unsalted butter, sprinkle with the chaat masala, coriander and red onion.

MAKES 10 FLATBREADS

1 bunch of fresh coriander (cilantro),
    finely chopped, plus extra to garnish
1 red onion, finely chopped, plus extra to garnish
1 recipe quantity Kulcha Dough (see page 19)
plain (all-purpose) flour, for dusting
250 g (9 oz/1 cup) unsalted butter, melted
a generous pinch of chaat masala per bread

FROM TOP TO BOTTOM:
LARDO KULCHA (SEE PAGE 25);
BUTTER KULCHA, CHILLI, GARLIC
& CHEESE KULCHA (SEE PAGE 24) AND
MASALA KULCHA (SEE RECIPE ABOVE)

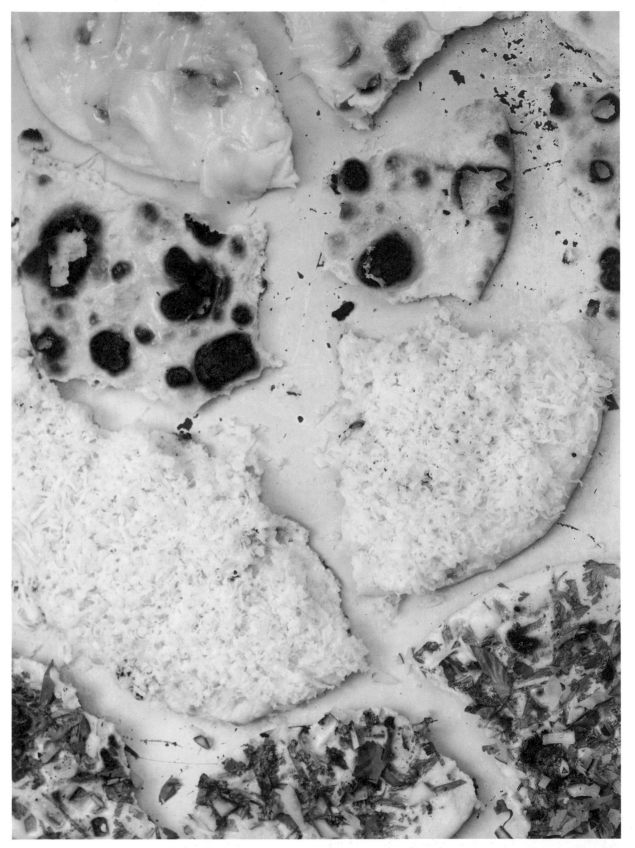

BREADS & SNACKS

BONE MARROW & CEP KULCHA

The bone marrow flavour can be subtle in this dish, so be brave and apply the butter liberally to the bread so that you get the full taste.

Soak the bones in cold water with a small handful of salt, ideally overnight.

Preheat the oven to 160°C (320°F/Gas 3).

Drain the bones and place in a roasting pan. Roast for about 15 minutes until just browned. Keep an eye on the bones or the marrow will melt.

Scoop out the bone marrow and measure the quantity. Place in a food processor and leave to cool to room temperature. Measure the butter and add at a ratio of 3:1 bone marrow to butter. Blitz until well blended.

Roll out the balls of dough on a lightly floured surface to about 15 cm (6 in).

Place the flatbreads, one at a time, on a hot, dry *tawa* or in a large frying pan (skillet) and cook for 3–4 minutes on each side until puffed up, lightly browned and charred in places.

Remove from the *tawa*, brush generously with the bone marrow butter and sprinkle with the cep powder. If using fresh ceps, thinly slice on a mandoline or using a sharp knife, and apply raw to the buttered kulcha. Season to taste with a little sea salt.

MAKES 10 FLATBREADS

1 kg (2 lb 3 oz) beef marrow bone
sea salt
approx. 150 g (5 oz/⅔ cup) unsalted butter, melted and cooled to room temperature
1 recipe quantity Kulcha Dough (see page 19)
plain (all-purpose) flour, for dusting
a generous pinch of cep (porcini) powder per portion, or 200 g (7 oz) fresh ceps (porcini), very thinly sliced

23

CHILLI, GARLIC & CHEESE KULCHA

Our version of a 'cheesy garlic naan', this bread sums up Kricket perfectly, matching the ever-popular garlic naan, with the Indian flavour combination of green chillies and the cheesy acidity of this artisanal British hard cheese. If you can't get Berkswell, you can try this with Parmesan, Pecorino, aged Cheddar, Comté or Gruyére. See recipe photo on pages 26–27.

Roll out the balls dough on a lightly floured surface to 15 cm (6 in) circles.

Place the flatbreads, one at a time, on a hot, dry *tawa* or in a large frying pan (skillet) and cook for 3–4 minutes on each side until puffed up, lightly browned and charred in places.

Remove from the pan, brush the bread generously with butter and sprinkle with the green chillies, garlic and grated cheese.

MAKES 10 FLATBREADS

1 recipe quantity Kulcha Dough (see page 19)
plain (all-purpose) flour, for dusting
100 g (3½ oz/generous ⅓ cup) unsalted butter melted
4 green chillies, finely chopped
4 garlic cloves, finely chopped
200 g (7 oz) Berkswell cheese, grated

LARDO KULCHA

Lardo is the cured back fat from a pig and is one of my favourite ingredients. It may not be a tradtional Indian ingredient, but it can be extremely versatile, and if served on top of bread, as shown on page 21, it provides a meatier, saltier alternative to butter. You should be able to buy lardo from your local butcher.

Roll out the balls of dough on a lightly floured surface to 15 cm (6 in) circles.

Place the flatbreads, one at a time, on a hot, dry *tawa* or in a large frying pan (skillet) and cook for 3–4 minutes on each side until puffed up, lightly browned and charred in places.

Remove from the tawa and place the sliced lardo onto the hot bread. The lardo will instantly melt over the bread as long as it is sliced thinly enough. There's no need for further seasoning as the fat is well seasoned in its curing process.

MAKES 10 FLATBREADS

1 recipe quantity Kulcha Dough (see page 19)
plain (all-purpose) flour, for dusting
200 g (7 oz) lardo, as thinly sliced as possible

25

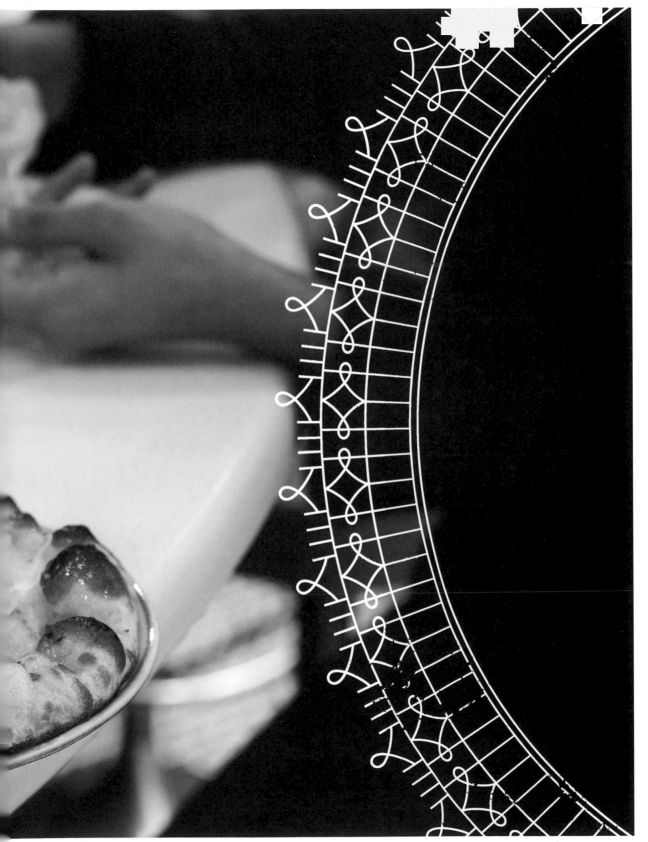

27

CHAPATI

An Indian household staple, chapatis are used as a vehicle for many a meal across the country. Typically served with dal and rice, chapatis or rotis can take their place alongside any Indian meal where there is a pickle or a sauce to eat it with.

Put the flour and salt in a large mixing bowl, then gradually add the water, mixing by hand until the dough is smooth and firm. Add the vegetable oil and mix by hand until incorporated into the dough. Cover with a damp cloth and leave to rest for 30 minutes at room temperature, then the dough can be set aside in the refrigerator until needed.

Portion the dough into 50 g (2 oz) balls, which will give you 8 small to medium-size chapatis. Roll out the dough to a few millimetres thick, and cook, one at a time on a hot, dry *tawa* or large frying pan (skillet). Cook the chapatis for about 2 minutes on each side until slightly browned or charred on top. Serve straight away.

MAKES 8 CHAPATIS

450 g (1 lb/3 cups) chapati or wholewheat or plain (all-purpose) flour, plus extra for dusting
1 teaspoon sea salt
250 ml (8½ fl oz/1 cup) filtered cold water
3 tablespoons vegetable oil

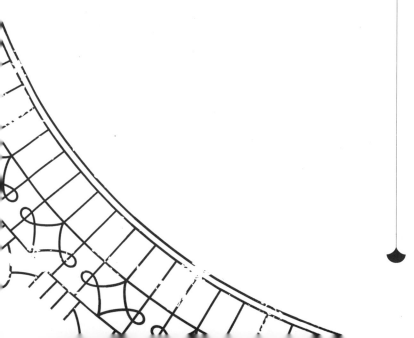

MASALA PAPAD

I remember eating these papads – or popadoms – in Delhi, with masala peanuts and a cold Kingfisher beer ... the perfect pre-meal warm up. Buy ready-made papads from your local Inidan supermarket, as they are the most authentic tasting.

Pour some vegetable oil in a heavy-based saucepan to a depth of roughly 1 cm (½ in), and heat until it is about 180°C (350°F). If you don't have a cooking thermometer, the oil is hot enough when a cube of bread sizzles when dropped into it.

Add the papads, one by one, and shallow-fry for a few minutes until they have crisped up and turned light brown. Remove from the oil and drain on kitchen paper.

Alternatively, hold the papad directly over a naked flame of a burner on your hob, moving and flipping them every few seconds, with a pair of tongs, until puffed up and slighly charred. They can also be cooked in the grill. Just keep a close eye on them as they puff and char very quickly!

Sprinkle the hot papads with the remaining ingredients and serve with the chutney.

SERVES 10

vegetable oil, for deep-frying
10 good-quality, store-bought papads
2 red onions, finely chopped
3 green chillies, finely chopped
2 bunches of fresh coriander (cilantro),
  finely chopped
a pinch of chaat masala per papad
Coriander Chutney (see page 195), to serve

31

NUT &
CURRY LEAF
MASALA

Macadamia nuts are my favourite, but they can be costly so do feel free to replace them with any other kind of nut. If you don't have jaggery, you could use caster (superfine) sugar instead, although, the jaggery adds a nutty, caramel-like taste and texture that you can't get with regular sugar, so if you can get your hands on it, I highly recommend it. This snack is seriously addictive so be sure you make plenty!

Preheat the oven to 180°C (350°F/Gas 4).

Combine all the ingredients, except the chaat masala, in a large bowl, tossing and stirring to make sure all the nuts are well coated in the spices.

Spread them evenly across a large baking tray and roast in the oven for about 8–10 minutes, or until the nuts are nice and golden. Give them a shake every 5 minutes or so to ensure they don't stick to the tray.

Remove from the oven and sprinkle with the chaat masala. Allow to cool, then serve.

SERVES 4

200 g (7 oz/1¼ cups) macadamia nuts
200 g (7 oz/1⅓ cups) cashew nuts
1 tablespoon ground turmeric powder
2 tablespoons Kashmiri red chilli powder
2 tablespoons garam masala
200 g (7 oz) jaggery, roughly chopped
50 g (2 oz/generous ⅓ cup) sea salt
80 g (3 oz) fresh curry leaves
50 g (2 oz) chaat masala

PEANUT & POMEGRANATE POHA

I enjoyed this dish most mornings in the restaurant in Mumbai. It's a staple breakfast item, particularly in the south of India. Poha is dried, flattened rice that can be prepared in many ways. It is available in most Indian supermarkets. Here is a fast and easy version that you can easily master at home. It goes perfectly with a hot cup of masala chai (see page 224). Give it a go!

Soak the poha in lukewarm water for 30 seconds to soften the rice, then drain.

Heat the oil in a large pan. Add the mustard seeds and fry for 30 seconds or so until they start to splutter. Add the curry leaves, turmeric and tomatoes, stir, then let it cook for about 2 minutes until the tomatoes have soften slightly, but still hold their shape.

Add the poha to the pan and stir continuously for a further 2 minutes until thoroughly combined with all the spices, then remove the pan from the heat.

Just before serving, add the roasted peanuts, lime juice, coriander and pomegranate seeds. Season to taste with a little salt, if necessary.

SERVES 4

400 g (14 oz) store-bought poha
1 tablespoon vegetable oil
2 tablespoons black mustard seeds
160 g (5½ oz) fresh curry leaves
1 tablespoon ground turmeric
2 tomatoes, deseeded and finely chopped
200 g (7 oz/1¼ cups) whole peanuts, roasted
juice of 2 limes
1 large bunch of fresh coriander (cilantro), finely chopped
1 pomegranate, halved and seeds scooped out
sea salt, to taste

EGG BHURJI WITH BERKSWELL & SHALLOTS

This dish was created almost by accident after we started making staff breakfast meals in our Soho restaurant. The first time I ate Indian scrambled eggs (or 'egg bhurji' in Mumbai) I remember thinking how superior it was to how we eat them at home – I found the Indian spices far more exciting. I have created my own version for you to try, but have stuck to the traditional way of preparing the eggs, using lots of butter, and cooking over a low heat, to retain that melt-in-the-mouth texture. With the lardo (cured pig fat), melting over the hot eggs, topped with salty Berkswell sheep's cheese and sweet and sour shallots, this is the perfect balance of flavours. If you can't get Berkswell, you can use Parmesan, Pecorino, aged Cheddar, Comté or Gruyére. Leave out the lardo if you're vegetarian – the result is still delcious!

36

To make the pickled shallots, steep the shallots in the pickling liquor for 1–2 hours at room temperature, then keep in the refrigerator until needed.

Whisk the eggs in a bowl with the red onion, green chillies and coriander.

Reserve a little of the butter for the toast and melt the remainder gently in a frying pan (skillet). Add the cumin seeds, curry leaves and turmeric and cook over a medium heat for 30 seconds or so, stirring, until the spices are fragrant.

Add the egg mixture, reduce the heat and cook very gently, stirring continuously with a spatula or a wooden spoon, for about 3–4 minutes until the eggs are just cooked but still soft. Season to taste with salt and remove from the heat.

Toast the sourdough bread and spread with the reserved butter. Spoon the egg mixture on the toast, top with a slice of lardo, a sprinkle of grated cheese, a few slices of the the pickled shallots and garnish with micro coriander leaves (if using).

SERVES 6

12 local, large free-range brown eggs
1 large red onion, finely chopped
3 green chillies, finely chopped
1 bunch of fresh coriander, finely chopped
200 g (7 oz/scant 1 cup) unsalted butter
1 tablespoon cumin seeds
1 handful of fresh curry leaves
1 teaspoon ground turmeric
4 slices of sourdough bread
12 slices of lardo
400 g (14 oz) Berkswell cheese, finely grated
sea salt, to taste
micro coriander (cilantro), to garnish (optional)

FOR THE PICKLED SHALLOTS

500 g (1 lb 2 oz) banana shallots, thinly sliced into rings
200 ml (7 fl oz/scant 1 cup) Pickling Liquor (see page 183)

NOTE: This recipe makes more pickled shallots than required for 4 people but it is well-worth making up a batch for you to use as you like! Just store in a sterilised jar and keep in the fridge. It will keep for a few months.

BREADS & SNACKS

FISH

Probably my favourite memory from my time in Mumbai was my first visit to the fish market in Sassoon Docks, the city's largest fishing port. It's best visited between four and six in the morning, and it's a fantastic way to see the organisation, skill and labour it takes to collect such a massive variety of fish and seafood. Every morning, fishermen return to the docks after being away for days, or even weeks at a time. They return to their wives who organise the catch to be sold on then and there or in the markets in the city later that day. If you can withstand the strong smell of fish as you enter the docks in the darkness, you will see an ancient industry in its most basic form. Amongst the multi-coloured boat lights bobbing around the pier, it is a beautiful sight, and one to be savoured and taken in. Go in silence, enjoy a chai at the edge and try not to get in the way of the fishermens' wives. They stop for no one!

HAKE WITH MALAI SAUCE

Despite the vast array of fish available in the Indian market, it can be difficult to get hold of super-fresh fish. This is often due to how the product is transported and treated once on dry land. Compensation for this lack of freshness often results in heavily spiced fish curries, where the true flavour of the fish cannot be identified. Back home, we have no such problem, and when it's super-fresh, I believe the best way to showcase the fish is to do as little to it as possible, and serve it with something that enhances the natural flavour of the fish you are using, rather than masking it. This recipe does exactly that.

Put the hake in a bowl, pour over the oil and sprinkle with the turmeric and a pinch of salt. Rub the fillets with the turmeric oil and leave to marinate.

To make the sauce, blitz the red onions in a food processor, until you have a smooth paste. Heat the oil in a pan, add the bay leaves and then the red onion purée. Cook over a medium heat, stirring frequently, for about 10 minutes until the water from the onions has evaporated and they have turned from purple to brown.

Add the ginger and garlic paste, cumin and turmeric and cook for a further 2 minutes.

Add the coconut milk and stir to a thick sauce consistency (the onion base will naturally thicken the sauce). Add the cardamom, coriander and lime juice, and season to taste with the salt and sugar.

Meanwhile, heat a little more oil in a pan and pan-fry the hake, skin-side down, over a medium to high heat for about 5 minutes until crispy. Flip the fish and add the samphire to the pan to warm through. At the same time, toss the poha in a hot, dry frying pan for 30 seconds or so until toasted.

Serve the fish and samphire on top of the malai sauce and sprinkle with the roasted poha to add texture to the dish.

SERVES 4

4 x 200 g (7 oz) hake fillets
4 tablespoons vegetable oil
a pinch of ground turmeric
a generous pinch of sea salt

FOR THE MALAI SAUCE

500 g (1 lb 2 oz) red onions, cut into chunks
150 ml (5 fl oz/scant ⅔ cup) vegetable oil,
  plus 1 tablespoon, for frying
2 fresh Indian bay leaves
2 tablespoons Ginger & Garlic Paste
  (see page 183)
2 tablespoons ground cumin
2 tablespoons ground turmeric
500 ml (17 fl oz/2 cups) coconut milk
1 tablespoon ground cardamom
1 tablespoon chopped fresh coriander (cilantro)
1 tablespoon lime juice
sea salt, to taste
caster (superfine) sugar, to taste
4 small handfuls of samphire
2 handfuls of poha

CLOCKWISE FROM THE TOP:
GRILLED SEA BREAM WITH COCONUT
& CORIANDER CHUTNEY (SEE PAGE 48);
OYSTERS IN COCONUT CREAM WITH GREEN
CHILLI GRANITA (SEE PAGE 52);
GRILLED LANGOUSTINES WITH
PICKLED TURMERIC
& LASOONI BUTTER
(SEE PAGE 51)

TORCHED MACKEREL WITH GOOSEBERRY CHUTNEY

This recipe is inspired by the flavours of Bengal, where fish and mustard have been used together for centuries. Here we are using mackerel, which must be super-fresh for this dish to taste its best. I prefer to cook the fish using a blow torch, so that it is remains a little raw in the middle, however a hot grill (broiler) will work just as well. If the fish is fresh, you shouldn't smell it at all, so take care in choosing wisely.

To make the pickled cucumber, steep the diced cucumber the in the pickling liquor for 1–2 hours, at room temperature, before putting in the fridge.

Prep the mackerel then mix together the oils, mustard, ginger and a pinch of salt in a bowl. Put the fish on a lined baking tray, spread the marinade over the flesh and leave for 30 minutes.

For the chutney, heat the oil in a large heavy-based saucepan, over a medium heat, stir in the onion seeds, bay leaf, chillies, and gooseberries. Turn the heat down and cook for 5 minutes. Add the turmeric, sugar and a little salt, to taste. Continue to cook until half the gooseberries are broken up and the other half remain whole. Remove from the heat and leave to cool.

Preheat the oven to 180°C (350°F/Gas 4).

Scatter the almonds on a baking tray, sprinkle over the chilli powder, if using, and shake to coat. Roast until browned and fragrant. Remove from the oven, toss with the chaat masala and allow to cool.

Take the tray of marinated mackeral and char the skin with a blow torch. The heat will refract from the tray underneath, allowing the fish to cook from both sides, leaving it slightly pink in the middle. Alternatively, you can use a grill (broiler). Arrange the fish on a plate, garnish with coriander leaves and serve with the gooseberry chutney, almonds and pickled cucumber.

SERVES 4

4 large mackerel fillets, bones removed
 and filleted in half
3 tablespoons mustard oil
3 tablespoons vegetable oil
3 tablespoons Kasundi mustard or other
 wholegrain mustard
a thumb-size piece of fresh ginger root, peeled
 and finely diced
a generous pinch of sea salt
50 g (2 oz/scant ½ cup) flaked (slivered)
 almonds
2 teaspoons Kashmiri red chilli powder (optional)
a pinch of chaat masala
a few coriander (cilantro) leaves,
 to garnish

FOR THE PICKLED CUCUMBER

1 cucumber, seeds discarded and diced
200 ml (7 fl oz/scant 1 cup) Pickling Liquor
 (see page 183)

FOR THE GOOSEBERRY CHUTNEY

2 tablespoons vegetable oil
1 teaspoon onion seeds
1 Indian fresh bay leaf
2–3 green chillies, finely chopped
200 g (7 oz) fresh or frozen gooseberries
1 teaspoon ground turmeric
100 g (3½ oz/scant ½ cup) caster
 (superfine) sugar
sea salt, to taste

CURED TROUT IN KASUNDI MUSTARD

Taking inspiration once again from the flavours of Bengal, this dish pairs fish with mustard. This time we use sea trout and give it a light cure. Wild sea trout is best, but if all you can get is farmed, that will also work. This is a more refined dish and should probably be served at the beginning of a special meal.

Begin by making the marinade. Combine the sugar, salt, lemon and lime zest, and chilli powder in a non-metal dish. Pour a little gin over the fillets, then place them flesh-side down in the marinade mix. Cover and set aside in the refrigerator for 8 hours. Turn the fillets over, re-cover and return to the refrigerator for a further 8 hours.

Rinse the fillets thoroughly under cold running water to remove any excess salt mixture. By this stage the fish should have cured slightly to the point where the flesh has lost most of its moisture and firmed up considerably. Pat dry with kitchen paper.

Lightly rub the flesh side of the fish with the mustard, cover and leave in the refrigerator until needed.

To make the pickled kohlrabi, steep the kohlrabi in the pickling liquor for 1–2 hours at room temperature, then keep in the refrigerator until needed.

To make the green pea purée, blitz the peas with the garlic, ginger, green chillies and mustard oil in a food processor, until you have a very smooth consistency. Season to taste with salt and sugar, cover and set aside in the refrigerator.

When ready to serve, slice the trout as thinly as you can, arrange on a plate and serve with the kohlrabi, and a small amount of the green pea purée.

SERVES 10

3–4 sea trout fillets (you can also use cod or salmon)
a splash of good-quality spiced gin
200 g (7 oz) Kasundi mustard or other wholegrain mustard

FOR THE MARINADE

500 g (1 lb 2 oz/scant 2¼ cups) caster (superfine) sugar
500 g (1 lb 2 oz/3¾ cups) sea salt
zest of 2 lemons
zest of 2 limes
200 g (7 oz/1⅔ cups) Kashmiri red chilli powder

FOR THE PICKLED KOHLRABI

2 kohlrabi, peeled and diced
400 ml (14 fl oz/generous 1½ cups) Pickling Liquor (see page 183)

FOR THE GREEN PEA PURÉE

450 g (1 lb/3½ cups) bag of frozen petits pois (baby sweet peas), defrosted
4 garlic cloves, peeled
a thumb-size piece of fresh ginger root
3 green chillies
100 ml (3½ fl oz/scant ½ cup) mustard oil
caster (superfine) sugar, to taste
sea salt, to taste

GRILLED SEA BREAM WITH COCONUT & CORIANDER CHUTNEY

Sea bream is a beautifully flavoured and textured fish that works perfectly grilled (broiled) whole. Memories of lunches on the beach in Kerala of whole grilled fish in a variety of different marinades was the inspiration behind this dish. Ask your fishmonger to descale and gut the fish for you. Serve it whole with a large spoon to peel away the flesh from the bones after you present it at the table.

Start by tempering the spices for the coconut and coriander chutney. Heat 2 tablespoons of the oil in a large, heavy-based pan until hot. Add the mustard seeds, channa dal, curry leaves and chillies and stir for 30 seconds or so until they splutter. Remove from the heat and allow to cool to room temperature.

Start the marinade for the fish. In a large bowl, combine the vegetable oil with the ginger and garlic paste, onion, fennel, caraway seeds, turmeric and salt, and mix thoroughly. Place the fish in the bowl and coat in the marinade, then place on a large dish and cover. Leave in the refrigerator to marinade for about an hour.

To finish the chutney, blitz the coriander with the ginger, green chillies and coconut, in a food processor, then gradually add enough of the remaining oil until it has a thick and smooth consistency. Remove from the blender into a bowl, add the tempered spices and their cooking oil, then add the lemon juice and season with salt and sugar. Refrigerate until needed, but bring the chutney back to room temperature before serving.

Heat a griddle pan on a medium-high heat and add a little oil. Griddle the fish for about 4 minutes on each side then transfer the pan to a grill (broiler) and continue to cook the fish until just tender. Serve with wedges of lime and the chutney.

SERVES 4

400–500 g (14 oz–1 lb 2 oz) whole sea bream, gutted and descaled
1 lime, cut into wedges

FOR THE COCONUT & CORIANDER CHUTNEY

about 250 ml (8½ fl oz/1 cup) vegetable oil
1 teaspoon black mustard seeds
1 teaspoon channa dal (yellow chickpea lentils)
a handful of fresh curry leaves
2 dried Kashmiri red chillies
400 g (14 oz) fresh coriander (cilantro)
50 g (2 oz) fresh ginger root, peeled and grated
3 green chillies
200 g (7 oz) fresh or frozen coconut
3 tablespoons lemon juice
sea salt, to taste
caster (superfine) sugar, to taste

FOR THE MARINADE

1 tablespoon vegetable oil
2 tablespoons Ginger & Garlic Paste (see page 183)
1 teaspoon onion seeds
1 teaspoon fennel seeds
1 teaspoon caraway seeds
1 teaspoon ground turmeric
50 g (2 oz/generous ⅓ cup) sea salt

GRILLED LANGOUSTINES WITH PICKLED TURMERIC & LASOONI BUTTER

Fresh turmeric is now readily available from all good grocery shops, and when pickled, it takes on a completely different flavour profile; sweet and almost candy-like. It pairs well with langoustines and the spicy acidic butter that is spooned over at the end. This dish works equally well with lobster or prawns (shrimps), but we like to keep things low cost and local so we've opted for Scottish langoustines, which deserve to be far more popular than they are now. They are beautifully delicate and I hope we will be seeing a lot more of these langoutines on menus across the country.

First make the pickle. Peel the turmeric root into thin ribbons, and place into a bowl. Steep in the pickling liquor for 1–2 hours at room temperature, then keep in the refrigerator until needed.

Prepare the langoustines by cutting lengthways down the centre of each, keeping the head intact, and removing the intestinal thread. Marinate in the oil, turmeric and salt, then cover and set aside in the refrigerator.

Make the lasooni butter by blitzing the butter in a food processor with the coriander, garlic, green chillies, a squeeze of lime juice and salt.

Grill (broil) the langoustines under a high heat for 2–3 minutes on each side until just cooked. Alternatively, you can also cook the langoustines in a heavy-based frying pan (skillet) over a medium to high heat. Ensure you do not overcook them.

Melt the lasooni butter gently in a small frying pan to retain its vibrant colour. Squeeze in little more lime juice, then spoon it over the cooked langoustines. Garnish with pickled turmeric and serve.

SERVES 4

16 fresh or frozen langoustines, defrosted
2 tablespoons vegetable oil, to coat the
  langoustines
2 teaspoons ground turmeric
a generous pinch of sea salt

FOR THE PICKLED TURMERIC

200 g (7 oz) fresh turmeric root, peeled
100 ml (3½ fl oz/scant ½ cup) Pickling Liquor
  (see page 183)

FOR THE LASOONI BUTTER

200 g (7 oz/scant 1 cup) unsalted butter,
  at room temperature
a bunch of fresh coriander (cilantro)
5 garlic cloves, peeled
4 green chillies
a couple of squeezes of lime juice
a pinch of salt

OYSTERS IN COCONUT CREAM WITH GREEN CHILLI GRANITA

On my most recent trip to Goa, I was introduced to a new restaurant hidden amongst the trees, off the beaten path in the north. The menu here changes daily, according to what is on offer and fresh that day. Here I had my first experience of oysters in India, and the memory stuck with me. The local oysters were served raw with coconut and green chillies. We do the same in the restaurant, using native British oysters – Porthilly happen to be my favourites – with the addition of sweet little bits of pickled cucumber. To enhance the flavour of this dish, you can garnish the oysters with an oyster leaf, but they can be hard to come by, so if you can't find them, don't worry!

Begin by making the green chilli granita. Dissolve the sugar and salt in the water in a small heavy-based saucepan over a medium heat. Remove from the heat and allow to cool.

Add the green chillies and coriander to the cooled seasoned water and place in a blender and blitz to a paste. You should end up with a vibrant green mixture. Place in a plastic freeze-proof tub and place in the freezer. After 30 minutes, break up the crystals using a fork to stop it from solidifying. Do this for a few hours until you have the desired granita consistency.

To make the pickles, steep the cucumber in the pickling liquor for 1–2 hours at room temperature, then keep in the refrigerator until needed.

Open the oysters using an oyster knife, ensuring that you loosen the flesh from the shell but retaining all the liquid.

To serve, arrange the oysters on a platter and spoon a little coconut cream on top of each oyster, followed by a spoonful of the chilli granita and then a little pickled cucumber. Serve straight away.

SERVES 10

20 fresh oysters of choice
200 g (7 oz/scant 1 cup) coconut cream

FOR THE GREEN CHILLI GRANITA

100 g (3½ oz/scant ½ cup) caster
  (superfine) sugar
a pinch of sea salt
200 ml (7 fl oz/scant 1 cup) water
4 green chillies
2 bunches of fresh coriander (cilantro)

FOR THE PICKLED CUCUMBER

1 cucumber, deseeded and finely diced
100 ml (3½ fl oz/scant ½ cup) Pickling Liquor
  (see page 183)

LASOONI SCALLOPS WITH GOAN SAUSAGE & NORI

This recipe has been on our menu since we first opened in Brixton. It remains a firm favourite and therefore, had to be included in this book. Scallops are not traditionally used in Indian cooking, but I find they work perfectly when paired with the herby lasooni butter. The added spice-kick from the sausage gives this dish a real edge, and the nori works as a wonderful seasoning, enhancing the overall flavour and appeal. Goan sausage can be tricky to source (see page 85); a good-quality chorizo works just as well.

Make the lasooni butter according to the instructions on page 51.

Prepare the scallops by gently removing the meat from the shell and discarding the attached muscle, skirt and black stomach sack but keeping the roe attached.

Heat a little of the oil in a large frying pan (skillet) and gently fry the sausage for about 4–5 minutes until lightly browned, then remove from the pan and set aside.

Reheat the pan over a medium heat. Season each scallop with a little oil and some salt, then add them to the hot pan, salt-side down. Fry for a few minutes until you get nice, golden colour on the underside. Turn the scallops over and remove the pan from the heat. Add the lasooni butter to the pan with another squeeze of lime juice and spoon each scallop with the buttery sauce.

To serve, place 3 scallops on each plate, and drizzle over any excess sauce from the pan. Garnish with the cooked sausage and sprinkle over poha and nori. Serve straight away.

SERVES 4

Lasooni Butter (see page 51)
12 fresh scallops with roes
2 tablespoons vegetable oil
200 g (7 oz) Goan sausage or
   chorizo, finely chopped
sea salt, to taste
a squeeze of lime juice
100 g (3½ oz) puffed rice, to sprinkle
10 nori sheets, finely sliced, to garnish

CORNISH CRAB MEEN MOILEE WITH TOASTED PEANUTS

Another dish that has stood the test of time on our menus; the choice of greens vary according to the seasons. It is a fresh take on the classic meen moilee Keralan curry. The meen — in this case, fish — is fresh white crab meat. Its sweetness works nicely with the spicy sauce, while the frisée lettuce adds freshness and bitterness to the dish.

To make the sauce, heat the coconut oil in a large heavy-based saucepan, then add the mustard seeds and heat for 30 seconds or so until they start to splutter. Add the curry leaves, then turn down the heat to low. Stir in the onions and cook for about 10 minutes until they are soft and translucent but without any colour.

Add the turmeric, green chillies and ginger and cook for a couple more minutes, stirring occasionally, so that onions are fully coated in the spices.

Finish the sauce with the coconut milk, cover and bring to the boil. Remove the pan from the heat and add the lime juice, coriander, sugar and salt. Taste and add more seasoning if required. Leave to cool completely, then transfer the sauce to the refrigerator.

Meanwhile, toss the peanuts in a dry frying pan (skillet) over a medium heat for a couple of minutes until lightly browned, then roughly chop and leave to one side.

When you are ready to serve, fold the crab meat and lettuce into the sauce. Add a little more lime juice, if necessary. Combine thoroughly and serve in bowls sprinkled with the toasted peanuts.

SERVES 4

400 g (14 oz) unpasteurised white crab meat

FOR THE SAUCE

2 tablespoons coconut oil
1 tablespoon black mustard seeds
a handful of fresh curry leaves
2 onions, thinly sliced
1 teaspoon ground turmeric
4 green chillies, chopped
2 thumb-size pieces of fresh ginger root, peeled and finely chopped
300 ml (10 fl oz/scant 1¼ cups) coconut milk
100 ml (3½ fl oz/scant ½ cup) lime juice, plus extra for serving
1 bunch of fresh coriander (cilantro), finely chopped
a pinch of caster (superfine) sugar
a pinch of sea salt
200 g (7 oz/1¼ cups) shelled unsalted peanuts
1 head of frisée lettuce (or lettuce of choice), washed and roughly chopped

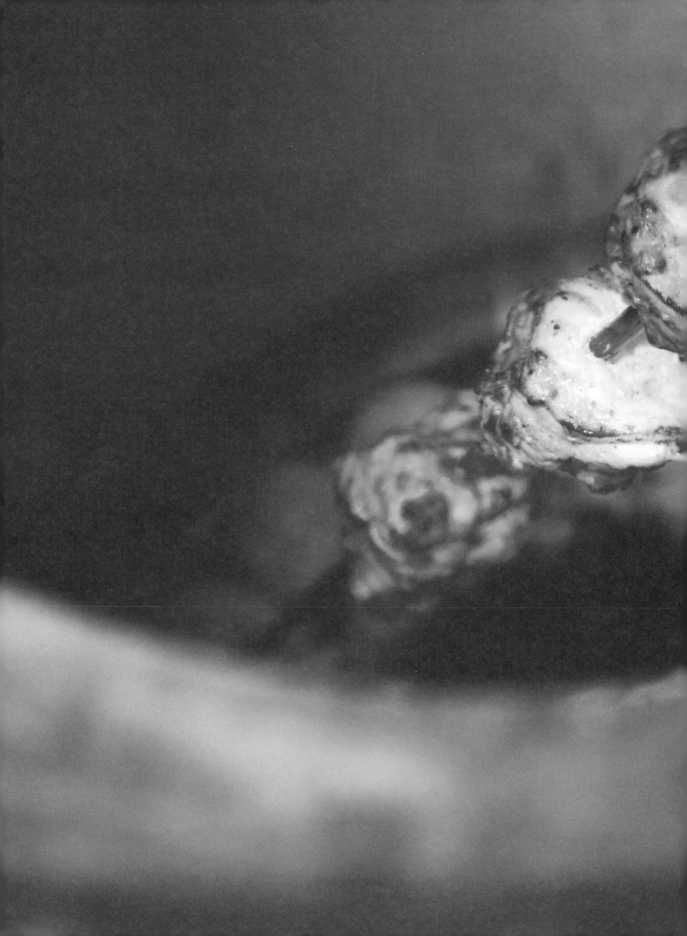

MARINATED TANDOORI MONKFISH WITH GREEN MANGO CHUTNEY

Monkfish is a very meaty fish and lends itself well to strong flavours. The marinade for this dish is punchy, but it won't permeate the fish entirely. In the restaurant, we cook this in the tandoor at around 300°C (572°F). I suggest you use a very hot grill (broiler), turning the fish frequently to stop it from burning too much on the outside. You can finish the fish off in a hot oven if it is taking on too much colour. It should be a little charred around the edges but not burnt.

Start by preparing the marinade. To hang the yoghurt, turn it out of its packaging straight into a muslin (cheesecloth), tie the ends and hang it over a dish for 1 hour. Make sure the yoghurt isn't stirred or disturbed otherwise you will lose it through the muslin. When the yoghurt is ready, remove from the muslin and place in a bowl with the remaining marinade ingredients and stir together. Add the monkfish and gently coat in the marinade then cover and set aside in the refrigerator for a few hours.

To make the chutney, heat 2 tablespoons of the oil in a large, heavy-based pan until hot. Add the mustard seeds, channa dal, curry leaves and the dried chillies and stir for 30 seconds until they splutter. Remove from the heat and allow to cool.

Blitz the remaining chutney ingredients in a blender, then add the remaining oil, until the mixture has a thick consistency. Remove from the blender into a bowl, add the tempered spices and their cooking oil, then season to taste with salt and sugar. Refrigerate until needed, but bring the chutney back to room temperature before serving.

Grill (broil) the monkfish under a medium heat for about 4 minutes on each side, ensuring that it takes a good colour on the outside and is just cooked in the middle. If the fish is browning too quickly under the grill, transfer it to a hot oven. Finish with chaat masala and lemon juice. Serve with the green mango chutney and lime wedges.

SERVES 4

600 g (1 lb 5 oz) monkfish fillet, cut into pieces
4 pinches of chaat masala
a small squeeze of lemon juice
1 lime, cut into wedges

FOR THE SPICED MARINADE

200 g (7 oz/scant 1 cup) Greek yoghurt
50 g (2 oz) Ginger & Garlic Paste (see page 183)
3 tablespoons mustard oil
1 teaspoon onion seeds
1 teaspoon fennel seeds
1 teaspoon caraway seeds
1 tablespoon ground turmeric
100 g (3½ oz) dried fenugreek leaves
25 g (1 oz/generous ¼ cup) sea salt

FOR THE GREEN MANGO CHUTNEY

150 ml (5 fl oz/scant ⅔ cup) vegetable oil
1 teaspoon yellow mustard seeds
1 teaspoon channa dal (yellow chickpea lentils)
a small handful of fresh curry leaves
2 dried Kashmiri red chillies
400 g (14 oz) fresh coriander (cilantro)
a thumb-size piece of fresh ginger root
3 green chillies
200 g (7 oz) fresh or frozen coconut pieces
4 garlic cloves, peeled
1 unripe peeled green mango, stone removed
  and flesh chopped
sea salt, to taste
caster (superfine) sugar, to taste

KARNATAKAN MUSSELS

On a food trip to Mumbai I discovered a seafood restaurant called Jai Hind (Lunch Home) where I tasted some of the best seafood I've had in the city to date. The restaurant showcased regional seafood cooking from places like Karnataka on the west coast of India. I ate a clam dish there, and loved it so much I identified all the ingredients and recreated it with mussels as soon as I got home.

First make the masala. Heat the coconut oil in a frying pan (skillet) until hot, then add the mustard seeds and heat for 30 seconds or so until they start to splutter. Add the curry leaves, reduce the heat to low and add the diced onions. Continue to cook for 10 minutes, stirring occasionally, until the onions are translucent but without any colour.

Add the turmeric, chilli powder, coconut, ginger and green chillies and season to taste with salt. Cook, stirring, for a couple minutes until fragrant. Continue to simmer on a low heat while you prepare the mussles.

Wash the mussels thoroughly and discard any that remain open when you tap them. Heat up a large heavy-based saucepan and add the wine. Let it simmer for a few minutes before adding the mussels. Cover tightly with a lid, and cook for about 4 minutes until the mussels have opened. Discard any that remain closed. Stir in the masala making sure the mussels are fully coated in all the spices.

To serve, spoon the mussles into 4 bowls and garnish with fresh coriander and lime juice to finish. Serve straight away.

SERVES 4

1 kg (2 lb 3 oz) fresh mussels, scrubbed and debearded
6 tablespoons dry white wine
a handful of fresh coriander (cilantro), chopped
a generous squeeze of lime juice, to drizzle

FOR THE MASALA

2 tablespoons coconut oil
1 tablespoon black mustard seeds
a large handful of fresh curry leaves
2 onions, finely diced
1 tablespoon ground turmeric
1 tablespoon Kashmiri red chilli powder
200 g (7 oz) fresh or frozen grated coconut
2 thumb-size pieces of fresh ginger root, grated
3 green chillies, finely chopped
sea salt, to taste

BUTTER GARLIC CRAB

If you ever visit Mumbai as a tourist, one of the first restaurants that is always recommended is a place called Trishna in Kala Ghoda – its fame carried on this one dish alone. The buttery-sweet crab makes this indulgent dish hard to resist and I have also used a little brown crab meat, for added flavour. The papads (dusted with blitzed seaweed) are the perfect vehicle for scooping up all that delicious crab meat – this is definitely one to try out at home! You can also serve this with freshly baked bread, to mop up all the juices.

Heat a couple tablespoons of water in a large heavy-based saucepan until bubbling. Add the butter and stir over a medium heat so an emulsion is formed.

Stir in the garlic, green chillies and black pepper and cook for a few seconds before adding the white and brown crab meat.

Cover and cook for 5 minutes, until the crab meat has absrobed most the liquid and the consistency is creamy and smooth. Remove the pan from the heat and finish with lime juice and coriander. Season to taste with salt.

Spoon the crab into bowls and serve with papads dusted with nori powder.

SERVES 4

150 g (5 oz/scant ⅔ cup) unsalted butter
4 tablespoons minced garlic
3 teaspoons finely chopped green chillies
4 teaspoon cracked black pepper
350 g (10½ oz) picked white crab meat
40 g (1½ oz) picked brown crab meat
2 tablespoons lime juice
a small handful of coriander (cilantro) leaves
sea salt, to taste

TO SERVE

4 store-bought papads or freshly baked bread
10 sheets nori, blitzed to a powder (optional)

65

SMOKED HADDOCK KICHRI

Kedgeree, or what we know it to be, was inspired by the Indian staple of kichri, which is a mixture of rice and lentils. Here we take the humble kichri, and familiarise it with smoked haddock and egg. The pickled cauliflower helps to provide a sharp contrast to the richness of the kichri, as well as added texture and crunch. (The recipe makes more than you'll need but you can store the rest in an airtight jar and use it within a few weeks.) If you prefer, you can serve the kichri with a poached egg rather than a raw, egg.

Start by pickling the cauliflower. Finely slice the cauliflower and add it to the pickling liquor. Steep for 1–2 hours then store in a sterilised jar, in the refrigerator.

To slow poach the haddock, pour the milk into to a heavy-based saucepan, along with the bay leaves and peppercorns. Bring to a simmer over a low heat and then add the haddock, skin-side down. Poach for about 10 minutes. Strain off the liquid and spices, cool and flake the flesh, discarding any bones and skin.

To make the kichri, put the moong dal in a saucepan and cover with cold water. Add the turmeric, bring to the boil then simmer for about 10 minutes until the lentils have completely cooked down and all the water has been absorbed. Leave to cool, then purée in a food processor.

Heat the oil in another saucepan, add the onion and cook over a medium heat until soft and translucent. Add the cumin, garlic, green chillies and ginger and stir before adding the lentil purée, cooked rice, poached haddock and butter. Mix gently, until everything is combined. Don't over-stir, as the fish will break. Add a little stock or water and more butter, if required – it should be creamy and luxurious. Remove from the heat and season to taste with salt. Spoon into bowls, top with a raw egg yolk and serve with the pickled cauliflower, coriander and black pepper.

SERVES 4

about 350 ml (12 fl oz/scant 1½ cups) full-fat (whole) milk
2 fresh Indian bay leaves
a few black peppercorns
300 g (10½ oz) un-dyed smoked haddock
4 large free-range egg yolks, to serve
a handful of coriander (cilantro) cress, to garnish
freshly ground black pepper, to garnish

FOR THE PICKLED CAULIFLOWER

1 small cauliflower
200 ml (7 fl oz/scant 1 cup) Pickling Liquor (see page 183)

FOR THE KICHRI

200 g (7 oz/scant 1 cup) yellow moong dal (lentils)
2 teaspoons ground turmeric
2 tablespoons vegetable oil
1 small onion, chopped
2 teaspoons cumin seeds
2 teaspoons finely chopped garlic
2 green chillies, finely chopped
2 teaspoons peeled and finely chopped fresh ginger root
400 g (14 oz/generous 2 cups) cooked and cooled basmati rice
100 g (3½ oz/scant ½ cup) unsalted butter, diced
sea salt, to taste
a little fish stock or water (if required)

CRAB SCOTCH EGG WITH MOILEE SAUCE

The Scotch egg is a quintessential British pub snack that has been given an Indian reinvention here, with the addition of spiced crab meat and a light, sweet and spicy moilee sauce. Make sure you time your boiled eggs to perfection, for maximum oozey, yolky goodness!

First make the moilee sauce. Heat the coconut oil in a large saucepan, then add the mustard seeds and cook until they start to splutter. Add the curry leaves, then turn down the heat before adding the onion. Cook for about 10 minutes until soft and translucent but without any colour. Add the turmeric, green chillies and ginger and stir to coat the onions in the spices. Pour in the coconut milk and bring to the boil, then remove from the heat. Add the lime juice and coriander, then season to taste with sugar and salt. Cover and leave to stand, ready to heat it up when you serve.

To make the Scotch eggs, bring a pan of salted water to the boil, lower 4 eggs into the water and simmer gently for 5 minutes. Remove the eggs from the water and place them straight into a bowl of iced water to stop them cooking. Once cooled, remove from the water, peel the eggs and set aside.

In a bowl, combine the white and brown crab meat together with the ginger, garlic, chillies, coriander and curry leaves. Shape the mixture around each egg. Beat the remaining 2 eggs in a bowl and put the flour and breadcrumbs into another. Roll the eggs first in the beaten eggs, followed by the flour and breadcrumbs mixture. Put the eggs into the refrigerator to firm up.

Pour the oil in a deep frying pan (skillet) or *kadai*, and heat until it is about 180°C (350°F). The oil is hot enough when a cube of bread sizzles when dropped into it. Lower the eggs, one by one, into the oil and fry for about 3–4 minutes until golden brown, then remove and drain on kitchen paper. Reheat the moilee sauce and serve with the Scoth eggs and the sautéed samphire.

SERVES 4

6 medium free-range brown eggs
160 g (5½ oz) unpasteurised white crab meat
80 g (3 oz) unpasteurised brown crab meat
1 tablespoon peeled and finely chopped fresh ginger root
1 tablespoon finely chopped garlic
1 tablespoon finely chopped green chillies
a handful of fresh coriander (cilantro), finely chopped
a handful of fresh curry leaves
200 g (7 oz/scant 2¾ cups) plain (all-purpose) flour
500 g (1 lb 2 oz/8 cups) panko breadcrumbs
1 litre (34 fl oz/4 cups) vegetable oil, for deep-frying
samphire, quickly sautéed in a little oil or butter, to serve

FOR THE MOILEE SAUCE

1 tablespoon coconut oil
1 teaspoon yellow mustard seeds
a handful of fresh curry leaves
1 large onion, chopped
1 tablespoon ground turmeric
2 green chillies, finely chopped
1 thumb-size piece of fresh ginger root, peeled and grated
200 ml (7 fl oz/scant 1 cup) coconut milk
a generous squeeze of lime juice
a handful of fresh coriander (cilantro), chopped
caster (superfine) sugar, to taste
sea salt, to taste

SEAFOOD BHEL
WITH NIMBU & SEV

I first came across this dish at a restaurant in Mumbai called the Bombay Canteen. The chef there takes pride in sourcing local seasonal produce and presenting it in a modern, non-pretentious way. It's a refreshing change in a city where so much is imported to cater for the middle class. I've adapted the basic recipe, using fresh local seafood. You'll find sev (a deep-fried chickpea-noodle snack seasoned with turmeric) in most Indian supermarkets.

Bring a large pan of well-salted water to the boil and blanch the squid rings and tentacles for for literally 20 seconds. Don't overboil as the squid will go tough and rubbery. Remove with a slotted spoon, place on kitchen paper and allow to cool.

To prepare the cockles, heat a large heavy-based saucepan until piping hot, throw in the cockles, add a splash of white wine, cover the pan and cook for a minute or so, shaking the pan occasionally, until all the cockles have opened. Discard any that remain closed. Pour the cockles onto a baking tray and allow to cool. Once the cockles are cool, pick the meat from the shells, place in a bowl and set aside in the refrigerator to cool completely.

To assemble the dish, place all the prepared seafood in a bowl and squeeze with the lime juice. Top with half the coriander, ginger, green chillies and chaat masala, and mix well. Season to taste with sugar and salt.

Just before serving, spoon the seafood into serving bowls, sprinkle with the sev and the remaining coriander. Eat straight away, before the sev gets soggy!

SERVES 4

200 g (7 oz) baby squid, cleaned and cut into rings, reserving the tentacles
200 g (7 oz) fresh cockles, cleaned
a splash of dry white wine
200 g (7 oz) cooked crayfish tails
a generous squeeze of lime juice
a handful of fresh coriander (cilantro), finely chopped
80 g (3 oz) fresh ginger root, peeled and finely chopped
2 green chillies, finely chopped
a generous pinch of chaat masala
caster (superfine) sugar, to taste
sea salt, to taste
200 g (7 oz) store-bought sev

COCKLE THORAN

Thoran is a traditional southern Indian dry curry, usually made with vegetables. Here we've replaced the usual veg with fresh cockles that have been cleaned, cooked and removed from their shells. You can also replace the cockles with clams, or even mussels. For the more traditional vegetarian option, use shredded cabbage instead of cockles.

Heat the oil in a large saucepan, add the mustard seeds and heat for 30 seconds or so until they start to splutter. Add the shallot and fry for 5 minutes until soft and translucent. Add the ginger and garlic paste and fry for a minute or so, stirring to mix everything together.

Stir in the coconut and the spices and cook for a couple of minutes, before adding the cockle meat. Mix well, coating the cockles fully in all the spices. Cover and cook for a few minutes until just tender.

Remove from the heat and season to taste with lime juice and salt. Spoon into bowls, garnish with curry leaves and serve.

SERVES 2

1 tablespoon vegetable oil
½ teaspoon black mustard seeds
1 banana shallot, finely chopped
1 teaspoon Garlic & Ginger Paste (see page 183)
150 g (5 oz) fresh or frozen grated coconut
½ teaspoon ground turmeric
1 teaspoon ground coriander
½ teaspoon cracked black pepper
½ teaspoon Kashmiri red chilli powder
1 teaspoon garam masala
200 g (7 oz) fresh cockles, scrubbed, cooked and removed from their shells (see page opposite)
a squeeze of lime juice
sea salt, to taste
a handful of fresh curry leaves, to serve

71

MACHER JHOL WITH PICKLED FENNEL

Macher Jhol is a traditional Bengali spicy fish curry, where we see the delicous flavour pairing of mustard with seafood. A simple fish stock will work for this recipe, although I prefer to make a langoustine bisque (by roasting the shells) to add an incredible depth and flavour to the dish. Palourde clams are small and sweet but you can use any clams if you can't obtain them. In fact, don't worry if you can't get hold of the exact fish used in the recipe – just use whatever is fresh and available to you. To make the mustard paste, simply grind your black mustard seeds with enough water, until you get a paste-like consistency.

First make the pickled fennel. Cover the sliced fennel with the pickling liquor and steep for 1–2 hours. Refrigerate until ready to serve.

To make the sauce, heat up a splash of the oil in a large saucepan over a medium heat, then add the cumin seeds and stir. Add the onions and cook for 10 minutes, stirring constantly, until translucent. Add 1 tablespoon of turmeric along with the mustard paste and chillies and cook for further 2 minutes. Add the tomatoes and lime juice, turn the heat down to low and simmer for about 5 minutes until the tomatoes have reduced by half and the sauce has thickened. Gradually add the fish stock to achieve a looser sauce consistency, then stir in the coriander and 1 teaspoon of salt. Keep the sauce simmering on a low heat while you prepare the fish.

Season the hake and mullet using the remaining oil, salt and turmeric. Pan-fry the fillets, skin-side only, to crisp up. (The fish will finish cooking in the broth.) Heat the wine in a saucepan over a high heat, add the clams, cover and cook for 3–4 minutes until they have opened up. Discard any that remain closed. Drop the langoustines in the hot tomato sauce, along with the fish, (skin-side up), and then the clams. Top with the pickled fennel and coriander before dishing out into bowls.

SERVES 4

4 x 80 g (3 oz) hake fillets
4 x 80 g (3 oz) red mullet fillets
8 langoustines, cut in half lengthways
  and intestinal vein removed
320 g (11 oz) Palourde clams, cleaned
100 ml (3½ fl oz/scant ½ cup) dry white wine
a handful of coriander (cilantro) cress, to garnish

FOR THE PICKLED FENNEL

1 bulb of fennel, thinly sliced
200 ml (7 fl oz/scant 1 cup) Pickling Liquor
  (see page 183)

FOR THE SAUCE

200 ml (7 fl oz/scant 1 cup) mustard oil
2 tablespoons cumin seeds
4 brown onions, thinly sliced
2 tablespoons ground turmeric
juice of 1 lime
200 g (7 oz) mustard paste
3 green chillies, split down the middle
1 kg (2 lb 3 oz) tomatoes, blitzed to a purée
1 litre (34 fl oz/4 cups) fish stock
a handful of fresh coriander (cilantro),
  finely chopped
2 teaspoons sea salt

SPICED COD'S ROE WITH TELICHERRY ROTI & PICKLED SHALLOTS

Telicherry peppercorns come from the Malabar region in Kerala. They are highly prized for their quality so do use them if you can find some in specialist Indian stores. If not, use any good-quality peppercorns. For extra flavour, you can garnish the spiced cod's roe with pickled yellow mustard seeds (see page 85).

To make the pickled shallots, steep the shallots in the pickling liquor for 1–2 hours at room temperature, then keep in the refrigerator until needed.

Remove the meat of the roe from the membrane and place in a blender. Discard the membrane. Squeeze the water from the bread, then add to the blender. Blitz on a slow speed, gradually pouring in the oil until the mixture is a smooth consistency. Scrape into a mixing bowl, then add the ground cumin, plenty of lime juice, then season with a little sugar and salt. Stir to combine and season further if required.

To make the chaptis, mix the peppercorns into the dough and roll out into 8 circles. Cook the chapati on a hot, dry *tawa*, or large frying pan (skillet) for 2 minutes on each side.

Garnish the spiced cod's roe with the pickled shallots then sprinkle with the chervil and serve with the warm chapatis.

SERVES 8

500 g (1 lb 2 oz) smoked cod's roe
100 g (3½ oz) stale sourdough bread,
    soaked in water
200 ml (7 fl oz/scant 1 cup) extra virgin olive oil
2 tablespoons cumin seeds, roasted and ground
juice of 1 lime
a pinch of caster (superfine) sugar
a pinch of sea salt
50 g (2 oz) fresh chervil leaves, to garnish

FOR THE CHAPATI

50 g (2 oz) Telicherry peppercorns,
    toasted and crushed (or whole white
    or black peppercorns)
1 recipe quantity Chapati Dough (see page 28)

FOR THE PICKLED SHALLOTS

200 g (7 oz) banana shallots
200 ml (7 fl oz/scant 1 cup) Pickling Liquor
    (see page 183)

AMRITSARI HADDOCK IN MUSTARD OIL

Amritsari fish pakoras are a popular street-food dish in the state of Punjab, in the north of India. They usually comprise of spiced fish coated in chickpea (gram) flour and fried street-side, then served with chutneys. Any fish can be used – such as cod or pollack – but in this case we use haddock. The addition of spiced peas and picked onions could almost make you feel like you're eating fish and chips. Almost...

To make the pickled shallots, steep the shallots in the pickling liquor for 1–2 hours at room temperature, then keep in the refrigerator until needed.

To make the marinade, toast the caraway, onion and fennel seeds in a dry frying pan (skillet) over a gentle heat for 30 seconds or so until they become fragrant, then set aside to cool. Transfer to a bowl then add the mustard oil, green chillies and ginger and garlic paste. Season to taste with sugar and salt, mix together then turn the fish in the marinade until it is completely coated. Cover and set aside in the refrigerator.

To make the pea purée, put the peas in a blender and blitz until you have a smooth, thick consistency, adding a little water if necessary.

To cook the fish, pour the oil in a heavy-based saucepan, and heat until it is about 180°C (350°F). The oil is hot enough when a cube of bread sizzles when dropped into it. Combine the cornflour, turmeric and chilli powder together in a bowl, and season with sugar and salt. Lightly dust the fish in the seasoned cornflour and carefully place into the hot oil, piece by piece. Cook for a couple of minutes until the fish pieces turn golden brown. Remove the fish from the oil and drain on kitchen paper.

Just before serving, sprinkle the fish with chaat masala, garnish with the pickled shallots and pea shoots and serve with the pea purée and pickled shallots.

SERVES 4

600 g (1 lb 5 oz) haddock, cut into 2.5 cm
(1 in) pieces
1 litre (34 fl oz/4 cups) vegetable oil
400 g (14 oz/3¼ cups) cornflour (cornstarch)
2 tablespoons ground turmeric
2 tablespoons Kashmiri red chilli powder
a generous pinch of chaat masala, to garnish
200 g (7 oz) pea shoots, to garnish
a pinch of caster (superfine) sugar
a pinch of sea salt

FOR THE PICKLED SHALLOTS

200 g (7 oz) banana shallots, thinly sliced
into rings
200 ml (7 fl oz/scant 1 cup) Pickling Liquor
(see page 183)

FOR THE MUSTARD MARINADE

1 teaspoon caraway seeds
1 teaspoon onion seeds
1 teaspoon fennel seeds
100 ml (3½ fl oz/scant ½ cup) mustard oil
2 green chillies, finely chopped
2 tablespoons Ginger & Garlic Paste
(see page 183)
caster (superfine) sugar, to taste
sea salt, to taste

FOR THE PEA PURÉE

500 g (1 lb 2 oz/3½ cups) frozen petit pois
(baby sweet peas), defrosted

GOAN
FISH
CURRY

This my updated take on the traditional Goan fish curry, with a slightly tangier taste and a thicker sauce consistency. You can use any firm white fish or shellfish you like, but here we find hake holds its shape rather well and the mussels are strong enough to take on the robust flavours of the sauce. If you prefer a runnier sauce, just add water or fish stock.

Begin by making the masala. Toast the fenugreek, coriander, cumin and fennel seeds with the fresh coconut in a dry frying pan (skillet). Keep the spices moving constantly over the heat for 30 seconds or so, and once the coconut takes on a light brown colour. Remove from the heat and allow to cool, then blitz in a food processor or blender to a fine paste.

Heat the oil in a deep pan, add the ginger and garlic paste and cook for 1 minute. Add the spice powder and cook over a low heat for a further 5 minutes before stirring in the turmeric. Cover and cook for further 2 minutes.

Stir in the fish stock, bring to the boil, then add the tamarind paste. Season to taste with the sugar and salt, then cover and cook for 5 minutes. Add the hake to the sauce, re-cover and cook gently for 3–4 minutes until the fish flakes easily.

Meanwhile, to prepare the mussels by washing them thoroughly. Heat a large heavy-based saucepan over a medium heat and add the wine. Quickly add the mussels, cover tightly with the lid, and cook for about 4 minutes until the mussels have opened. Discard any that remain closed.

Add the mussels to the masala sauce and mix thoroughly, cooking for a few more minutes. To serve, spoon the seafood into bowls and top with fresh coriander.

SERVES 4

300 g (10½ oz) hake fillets, cut into chunks
200 g (7 oz) mussels, scrubbed and debearded
a generous splash of dry white wine
a handful of fresh coriander (cilantro) leaves,
  to serve

FOR THE MASALA

1 tablespoon fenugreek seeds
1 tablespoon coriander seeds
1 tablespoon cumin seeds
1 tablespoon fennel seeds
200 g (7 oz) fresh or frozen grated coconut
1 tablespoon vegetable oil
2 tablespoons Ginger & Garlic Paste
  (see page 183)
2 teaspoons ground turmeric
200 ml (7 fl oz/scant 1 cup) fish stock
100 g (3½ oz/scant ½ cup) tamarind paste
caster (superfine) sugar, to taste
sea salt, to taste

MEAT

Meat in India generally comes in the form of chicken or goat (known as mutton). In some states, where there is more religious diversity – such as Goa and Kerala – pork is eaten in small pockets; beef has now become a banned product in the country. The quality of the meat available is often variable, which leads certain higher-end restaurants importing their meat from abroad. Unfortunately, poor treatment of animals and inferior transportation methods means that meat in India isn't always as fresh as it could be. Despite this, however, chefs and cooks across India are still able to make something extraordinary from something ordinary. If you try the chicken or mutton in kebab form, from street vendors, the overall flavour is still so delicious. Often with the addition of spices, vinegars, salt and particularly raw papaya, the meat that is used becomes far more tender, and over the centuries, Indian cooks have adapted in ways like this with fantastic results. In the West, we are fortunate enough to be able to source high-quality meat. At the restaurant, we source our meat only from the British Isles – the more local your meat, the better, so I encourage you to get to know your butcher and to use what is fresh and available near you.

GOAN SAUSAGE ROLL WITH PICKLED RED ONION & CURRY LEAF MAYO

We first served this dish as part of our brunch menu in Brixton, weeks after we opened, and it went down a storm. At the time, we sourced our Goan sausage from what was the only supplier in the UK, down in nearby Croydon. Now we make our own, but you can simply use a soft chorizo in its place. You'll find ingredients such as curry leaf powder, sev (see page 70) and frozen Malabar parathas in any good Indian stores and some mainstream supermarkets.

First, make the pickles. Pour a little of the pickling liquor over the mustard seeds and the remainder over the onions. Leave to steep for 1–2 hours at room temperature, then keep in the refrigerator until needed.

Grill (broil) or fry the sausages until nicely charred on the outside. If the sausages are cured or smoked, they need only a couple minutes cooking, otherwise cook all the way through.

Heat up a *tawa* or large frying pan (skillet), brush with a little vegetable oil then cook the parathas, one at a time, for 3–4 minutes on each side until the bread is golden brown. Brush the pan with a fresh coat of oil each time.

Assemble the sausage rolls by spreading a tablespoon of coriander chutney on one side of each paratha, followed by a tablespoon of chilli garlic mayonnaise. Place the sausages in the middle of the parathas and fold the bread around neatly, to form a roll. Cut off the ends to tidy it up. To serve, place one roll on each plate, garnish with the pickles and top with the sev and fried curry leaves. Serve with a tablespoon of the curry leaf mayonnaise on the side, and sprinkle over the curry leaf powder as photographed.

SERVES 4

4 Goan sausages or soft chorizo sausages
vegetable oil, to coat the pan
4 ready-made Malabar parathas
4 tablespoons Coriander Chutney (see page 195)
4 teaspoons Chilli Garlic Mayonnaise
  (see page 187)
50 g (2 oz) store-bought sev, to serve
80 g (3 oz) fresh curry leaves, fried until crisp,
  to serve
4 tablespoons Curry Leaf Mayonnaise
  (see page 200)
50 g (2 oz) curry leaf powder (ground dried curry
  leaves), to garnish

FOR THE PICKLES

200 ml (7 fl oz/scant 1 cup) Pickling Liquor
  (see page 183)
100 g (3½ oz) yellow mustard seeds
2 red onions, thinly sliced into rings

LAMB GALOUTI KEBAB WITH CHUTNEY & BURNT ONION RAITA

I tried my first galouti kebab in the side streets of the old city in Lucknow. After a starter of what was a suspiciously green lassi, I was led down the back streets into a restaurant that only served these special kebabs, with roomali roti (a paper-thin roti) to scoop it up with. I was immediately struck by the sheer tenderness of the meat, packed with flavour and with an almost pâté-like consistency. That experience has remained with me to this day, which is why you'll see often this kebab on our menus. I've added caul fat (lace fat), to help shape the meat before cooking, but this can be omitted if you can't get it from your butcher. The trick to this dish is to heavily season the mince with the various aromatic spices, and massage it for as long as possible. Trust me, the texture you will achieve from this will melt in your mouth and will be thoroughly worth the time spent. You can buy the kewra water, papaya paste and cashew nut butter ready-made, in most Indian stores.

To make the pickled shallots, steep the shallots in the pickling liquor for 1–2 hours at room temperature, then keep in the refrigerator until needed.

Combine the minced lamb, chilli powder, coriander, green chillies, garam masala, papaya paste, if using, cashew nut butter, onion paste, kewra water, rose water and saffron in a bowl and massage the flavourings into the meat until thoroughly combined. Put the mixture into a blender or food processor and blitz until completely smooth, seasoning with sugar and salt. Transfer the mix to the refrigerator. This will make it easier to handle the meat when you portion it.

Divide the mixture into 8 balls and flatten to the shape of a patty. Wrap in the caul fat, if using. Heat the oil in a heavy-based frying pan (skillet) and shallow-fry the kebabs over a medium heat for 3–4 minutes on each side until cooked through and browned. Remove from the pan and leave to rest for 2 minutes.

Garnish with mint and serve with the chutney, pickles and raita.

SERVES 4

500 g (1 lb 2 oz) lamb leg, minced (ground)
3 tablespoons Kashmiri red chilli powder
1 bunch of fresh coriander (cilantro), chopped
4 green chillies, finely chopped
3 tablespoons garam masala
2 tablespoons green papaya paste (optional)
2 tablespoons store-bought cashew nut butter
1 small onion, minced to a paste
2 tablespoons kewra water
2 tablespoons rose water
a pinch of saffron strands, soaked in warm water
a pinch of caster (superfine) sugar
1 teaspoon sea salt, plus more to taste
200 g (7 oz) caul fat (lace fat) (optional)
2 tablespoons vegetable oil
2 teaspoons chopped fresh mint, to serve
200 g (7 oz) Coriander & Mint Chutney
  (see page 185), to serve
Burnt Onion Raita (see page 216)

FOR THE PICKLED SHALLOTS
800 g (1 lb 12 oz) shallots, thinly sliced into rings
200 ml (7 fl oz/scant 1 cup) Pickling Liquor
  (page 183)

KERALAN FRIED CHICKEN

This dish came about almost by accident, and has proved to be arguably the most popular dish on our menu. When we first opened Kricket inside a shipping container in Brixton in 2015, I learnt quickly that there was to be no room for a tandoor, only a fryer. So I adapted a basic tandoori marinade, made use of our small gas fryer and Kricket's very own fried chicken was born. It is likely to remain on the menu for some time to come!

To make the spicy marinade, mix the yoghurt, buttermilk, chilli powder, turmeric, green chillies and coriander together in a bowl. Turn the chicken thighs in the marinade so it is coated, cover and leave in the refrigerator for about 2 hours.

To make the pickled mooli, steep the sliced mooli in the pickling liquor for 1–2 hours at room temperature, then keep in the refrigerator until needed.

Pour the vegetable oil in a deep frying pan (skillet) or *kadai*, and heat until it is about 180°C (350°F). The oil is hot enough when a cube of bread sizzles when dropped into it.

While the oil heats up, combine the flour, cornflour, chilli powder and turmeric in a shallow bowl.

Lift the chicken out of the marinade and coat in the flour-mix, shaking off any excess. Deep-fry in the oil for about 5 minutes until the outside is golden brown. To ensure the chicken is cooked through, test the middle of the biggest piece of chicken with a probe thermometer; it should be over 75°C (167°F).

Remove the chicken from the fryer and drain on kitchen paper. Sprinkle generously with chaat masala. Serve with the pickled mooli, fried curry leaves and the curry leaf mayonnaise.

SERVES 4

400 g (14 oz) boneless, skinless, free-range chicken thighs, cut into 2.5 cm (1 in) pieces
1 litre (34 fl oz/4 cups) vegetable oil, for deep-frying
100 g (3½ oz/generous ¾ cup) plain (all-purpose) flour
100 g (3½ oz/generous ¾ cup) cornflour (cornstarch)
1 tablespoon Kashmiri red chilli powder
1 tablespoon ground turmeric
a generous pinch of chaat masala per portion
80 g (3 oz) fresh curry leaves, lightly fried, to serve
200 g (7 oz/scant 1 cup) Curry Leaf Mayonnaise (see page 200), to serve

FOR THE SPICY MARINADE

300 g (10½ oz/1¼ cups) Greek yoghurt
100 ml (3½ fl oz/scant ½ cup) buttermilk
1 tablespoon Kashmiri red chilli powder
1 tablespoon ground turmeric
3 green chillies, finely chopped
1 bunch of fresh coriander (cilantro), finely chopped

FOR THE PICKLED MOOLI

200 g (7 oz) mooli (daikon), peeled and thinly sliced
200 ml (7 fl oz/scant 1 cup) Pickling Liquor (see page 183)

GANA'S PORK CHEEK COORG

A little while back, a customer came into the restaurant in the Soho restaurant for dinner and, on leaving, he introduced himself as Gana and thanked me for a wonderful meal. However, before leaving, he suggested we include a pork curry on our menu to make it complete, so I invited him in to cook one to see if we could recreate it for the restaurant. He cooked us his version of pork belly coorg, a dish that was common in his native state of Karnataka. Sure enough, it tasted delicious and what was equally appealing was Gana's enthusiasm towards this dish and what it meant to him. We've adapted the recipe slightly by using pork cheek rather than belly, as its gelatinous quality lends itself brilliantly to slow cooking, and we serve it with pickled fennel and a scattering of roasted peanuts. It's a delightfully comforting dish, and whenever the season calls for it, it will be on our menu. So thank you to Gana, for introducing us to this recipe; it's always great when a happy customer shows as much love for our dishes as we do. Gana, (now living in Melbourne, Australia) this one's for you!

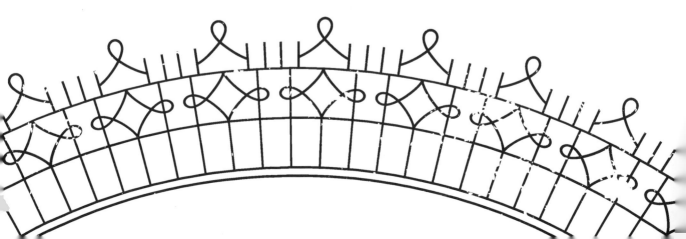

To make the pickled fennel, steep the fennel in the pickling liquor for 1–2 hours at room temperature, then keep in the refrigerator until needed.

To make the spice mixture, roast the whole spices and half of the curry leaves in a dry frying pan (skillet) over a low heat for 3–4 minutes. Alternatively, you can cook them in a preheated oven at 180°C (350°F/Gas 4) for about 10 minutes until fragrant and lightly browned. Allow the spices to cool before grinding to a powder.

To make the pork marinade, mix together the onions, green chillies, ginger and garlic paste, the remaining curry leaves, turmeric and chilli powder in a bowl. Turn the pork in the marinade so it is completely coated, then leave it for at least 4 hours or preferably overnight, in the refrigerator.

Heat the oil in a deep heavy-based saucepan and add the marinated pork and all the marinade juices. Cover and cook over a low heat for about 2 hours until the moisture in the onions has disappeared. Turn the heat down to minimum and continue to cook the pork for another 2 hours, topping up with a little hot water if you feel the mixture is getting too dry. The result should be a semi-dry curry, so make sure you don't add too much water so that the cheeks overcook. The meat is cooked when it simply flakes apart.

Stir in the spice mixture, malt vinegar, tamarind chutney and season to taste with salt. Serve hot, spooned intp bowls and garnished with the pickled fennel and roasted peanuts.

SERVES 4

8 pork cheeks
2 tablespoons vegetable oil
4 tablespoons malt vinegar
4 tablespoons Tamarind & Date Chutney
  (see page 184)
sea salt, to taste
100 g (3½ oz/⅔ cup) roasted unsalted peanuts,
  to serve

FOR THE PICKLED FENNEL

1 bulb of fennel, thinly sliced
200 ml (7 fl oz/scant 1 cup) Pickling Liquor
  (see page 183)

FOR THE SPICE MIXTURE

1 cinnamon stick
4 star anise
1 teaspoon cloves
1 tablespoon coriander seeds
1 teaspoon black peppercorns
4 green cardamom pods
1 teaspoon cumin seeds
1 teaspoon mustard seeds
½ teaspoon fenugreek seeds
80 g (3 oz) fresh curry leaves, finely chopped

FOR THE PORK MARINADE

6 red onions, puréed
4 green chillies, slit down the middle,
  seeds intact
6 tablespoons Ginger & Garlic Paste
  (see page 183)
2 tablespoons ground turmeric
2 tablespoons Kashmiri red chilli powder

DUCK BREAST WITH SESAME & TAMARIND SAUCE

The sauce in this recipe originates from Hyderabad and it pairs perfectly with the fatty duck breast and the sweet, acidic cucumber. Ideally, lay the duck on kitchen paper, uncovered in the refrigerator, overnight, to dry the breasts. I like the duck medium rare, but if you prefer it more well done, just increase the cooking and resting times accordingly.

First make the pickled cucumber by steeping the ribbons in the pickling liquor for 1–2 hours. Set aside in the refrigerator until needed.

Preheat the oven to 200°C (400°F/Gas 6).

Mix the chilli marinade ingredients together in a bowl, then turn the duck in the marinade and keep refrigerated until needed.

To make the stock, roast the bones in the oven for 30 minutes until nicely coloured. Transfer to a saucepan, add the remaining ingredients and cover with water. Bring to the boil, cover and cook over a low heat for an hour. Strain into a bowl, and set aside.

Make the masala by toasting the ingredients in a dry frying pan (skillet) until fragrant. Tip into a blender, add a little water and blitz to a paste.

Heat the oil in deep frying pan over a low heat and add the mustard and onion seeds and the curry leaves, then add the puréed onions and cook for 10 minutes until soft. Add the remaining ingrediets and mix together. Spoon in the masala and loosen with the duck stock. Season to taste and set aside.

Turn the oven down to 160°C (320°F/Gas 3). Place the duck skin-side down in a cold frying pan, then gradually increase the heat to render the fat and crisp the skin. Place the breasts in a baking tray and cook in the oven for 6 minutes. Remove, cover with foil, and leave to rest for 10 minutes. Cut the breasts in slices and serve on top of the sauce, and garnish with ribbons of pickled cucumber on the side. Drizzle with chilli oil.

SERVES 4

4 duck breast fillets, lightly scored
a splash of vegetable oil
4 teaspoons mustard seeds
2 teaspoons onion seeds (or Nigella seeds)
80 g (3 oz) packet of fresh curry leaves
4 onions, puréed
2 tablespoons ground turmeric
2 tablespoons Kashmiri red chilli powder
100 g (3½ oz/scant ½ cup) tamarind paste
sea salt, to taste
good-quality chilli oil, to serve

FOR THE CHILLI MARINADE

1 tablespoon Kashmiri red chilli powder
2 tablespoons vegetable oil
4 pinches of sea salt

FOR THE DUCK STOCK

500 g (1 lb 2 oz) duck bones
2 star anise
2 fresh Indian bay leaves

FOR THE MASALA

200 g (7 oz/1⅓ cups) cashew nuts
100 g (3½ oz/1⅔ cups) desiccated
  (dried shredded) coconut
5 cloves
100 g (3½ oz/⅔ cup) sesame seeds
4 teaspoons coriander seeds
4 teaspoons cumin seeds
2 teaspoons fenugreek seeds

FOR THE PICKLED CUCUMBER

2 cucumbers, halved, deseeded and ribboned
200 ml (7 fl oz/scant 1 cup) Pickling Liquor
  (see page 183)

KID GOAT RAAN

Raan is a northern Indian style of cooking meat, equivalent to our Sunday lunch, presented whole or — as we do in our restaurant — slow-cooked and shredded, it is rich and heavily spiced. If you can't get goat, try it with lamb leg or beef shin instead. I like to serve this with freshly chopped mint and a scattering of pomegranate seeds.

Rub the meat with the ginger and garlic paste, chilli powder and a pinch of salt and leave overnight to marinate.

Preheat the oven to 200°C (400°F/Gas 6).

Transfer the leg to a deep ovenproof pan, add the remaining spices and vinegar, then pour in the water (it should just cover the meat). Cover the pan and cook in the oven for 30 minutes. Lower the oven temperature to 160°C (320°F/Gas 3) and cook for a further 4–5 hours until the meat is falling off the bone.

Remove from the oven, take the meat out of the braising liquid and allow to cool. The meat is cooked when you can easily pick it from the bone. Transfer the braising liquid to a heavy-based saucepan and boil over a high heat until it has thickened and the flavours have intensified.At this point, strain the liquid into a separate pan, reduce the heat and add the cream, saffron and garam masala. Reduce for a further 5 minutes, adjust the seasoning to taste and set aside to cool.

When you are ready to serve, heat a large frying pan (skillet) over a high heat and sear off the goat to get a nice crispy exterior. Add the braising liquid to the pan and spoon the liquid over the meat until it coats it nicely. Serve the meat whole, in its braising liquid.

SERVES 10

1 kid goat leg
4 tablespoons Ginger & Garlic Paste (see page 183)
2 tablespoons Kashmiri red chilli powder
a pinch of sea salt
2 fresh Indian bay leaves
3 star anise
1 teaspoon black peppercorns
1 teaspoon cloves
1 cinnamon stick
400 ml (14 fl oz/generous 1½ cups) white distilled vinegar
about 1.6 litres (56 fl oz/6⅔ cups) cold water
500 ml (17 fl oz/2 cups) double (heavy) cream
a generous pinch of saffron strands, soaked in a little warm water
3 tablespoons garam masala

95

CLOVE-SMOKED WOOD PIGEON WITH CHANTERELLES & PEAS

Indian food pairs fantastically with game, and towards the end of the year we try to include as many different game dishes at the restaurant, as possible. Wood pigeon is luckily available throughout the year, and this dish has been a permanent fixture on our menu for some time now. What makes it special to me is the addition of the French pigeon sauce, elevated with some whole spices, and combined with the masala to form the base for the pigeon. As with all game birds we use, we try to cook the whole bird, and this dish is no exception.

Preheat the oven to 180ºC (350ºF/Gas 4).

First remove the breasts of the pigeons. Roast the rest of the carcasses in a rosting pan for about 40 minutes until nicely browned. Set aside.

Toast the pigeon spice mix ingredients in a dry frying pan (skillet) for a few minutes until fragrant, tossing the pan occasionally, then blitz to a fine powder in a food processor.

In a bowl, combine the spice mix with the oil, ginger and garlic paste, chilli powder and salt to make the marinade. Turn the pigeon breasts in the marinade until fully coated, then leave to one side until required.

To make the pigeon stock, heat the oil in a large, heavy-based sauce pan and add the cloves, peppercorns and bay leaves and fry for 30 seconds or so. Add the carrot, onions, celery and garlic and cook on a medium to high heat for 10 minutes, stirring constantly, until nicely caramelised. Deglaze the pan with the white wine and stir to mix in the spices, then add the pigeon carcasses. Top up with water to cover, bring to the boil, then reduce the heat, cover and cook for at least 2 hours to infuse the flavours into the stock.

continued overleaf

SERVES 4

4 whole wood pigeons, skin on
150 g (5 oz) Pumpkin Chutney (see page 208),
  to serve
a handful of fresh coriander (cilantro), chopped,
  to serve

FOR THE PIGEON SPICE MIX

1 tablespoon cumin seeds
1 tablespoon black peppercorns
½ tablespoon cloves

FOR THE MARINADE

2–3 tablespoons vegetable oil
4 tablespoons Ginger & Garlic Paste
  (see page 183)
1 tablespoon Kashmiri red chilli powder
a pinch of sea salt

FOR THE PIGEON STOCK

2 tablespoons vegetable oil
½ teaspoon cloves
1 teaspoon black peppercorns
3 fresh Indian bay leaves
1 carrot, roughly chopped
2 onions, finely chopped
a few sticks of celery, roughly chopped
1 bulb of garlic, peeled
100 ml (3½ fl oz/scant ½ cup) white wine

Strain the stock through a fine sieve, then return the liquid to the saucepan and boil until it has reduced by half.

To make the onion and tomato masala, heat 2 tablespoons of the vegetable oil in a small pan, add the cumin seeds and cook for a minute or so to allow the spice to infuse the oil. Then add the onions and fry for about 15–20 minutes until nicely caramelised. Add the ginger and garlic paste, stir for a few seconds before adding the tomatoes, and cook for 10–15 minutes until the tomatoes have reduced and you are left with a thick sauce. Finally add the peas, stir then remove the pan from the heat.

To prepare the mushrooms, melt the butter in a separate frying pan (skillet) with an equal quantity of water, add the chanterelles and cook for about 3–4 minutes until almost cooked. Then add them tomato masala, along with a little pigeon stock. Season to taste with salt.

Cook the marinated pigeon breasts under a hot grill (broiler) for a couple of minutes on each side and then leave to rest for 4 minutes. The breasts should be rare to medium rare.

To serve, reheat the masala until hot then spoon onto the plates. Arrange the pigeon breasts on top and serve with pumpkin chutney and freshly chopped coriander.

FOR THE ONION AND TOMATO MASALA

4 tablespoons vegetable oil
1 teaspoon cumin seeds
2 brown onions, diced
2 tablespoons Ginger & Garlic Paste
  (see page 183)
400 g (14 oz) tomatoes, puréed
150 g (5 oz/1 cup) fresh podded peas

FOR THE MUSHROOMS

75 g (2½ oz/generous ¼ cup) unsalted butter
250 g (9 oz) chanterelle (girolle) mushrooms

99

AFGHANI QUAIL WITH SHALLOT & GINGER RAITA

You can ask your butcher to spatchcock the quail but it is easy to do it yourself. Lay the bird breast-side down on a board, take a knife and remove just the backbone, then turn it over and gently press down on the breast to flatten the bird.

First make the marinade. Toast the melon and poppy seeds in a dry frying pan over a medium heat for 3 minutes until fragrant and lightly browned. Allow the spices to cool, then using a food processor, blitz to a powder.

Mix the spices with the cream, cashew butter, oil, pepper, cheese, cardamom, ginger and garlic paste and saffron. Mix well, then add the quail, cover and leave to marinate in the refrigerator for at least 12 hours, preferably overnight.

When you are ready to cook, heat the grill (broiler) to hot, and cook the marinated quail, skin-side down first, for about 4 minutes on each side. The bird should have good colour on it but not too much, so If you feel it's getting burnt, then you can transfer it to a hot oven for 5 minutes to complete the cooking process.

Once the quails are cooked, brush with melted butter, squeeze over the lime juice and season with chaat masala. Leave to rest for about 10 minutes, then serve with the shallot and ginger raita and some rice.

SERVES 4

4 x whole quail, spatchcocked
2 tablespoons melted butter
a good squeeze of lime juice
a generous pinch of chaat masala
200 g (7 oz) Shallot & Ginger Raita
   (see page 204), to serve
cooked basmati rice, to serve

FOR THE MARINADE

2 tablespoons melon seeds
2 tablespoons white poppy seeds
200 ml (7 fl oz/scant 1 cup) double
   (heavy) cream
2 tablespoons store-bought cashew butter
3 tablespoons vegetable oil
1 tablespoon freshly ground black pepper
150 g (5 oz/1¼ cups) Cheddar cheese,
   grated
1 teaspoon ground cardamom
2 tablespoons Ginger & Garlic Paste (see page 183)
a pinch of saffron strands, soaked in a little
   warm water

SULLA RUMP OF VENISON WITH CHUTNEY & ARTICHOKE CRISPS

The aromatic marinade used on the meat here should add several layers of flavour to the overall dish. Be careful not to cook the meat on too high a flame otherwise the spices will burn. We like to serve the venison medium rare, but it can be cooked however you like. Bear in mind, as it's a very lean meat, it will tend to dry out if cooked for too long.

To hang the yoghurt, turn it out of its packaging straight into a muslin (cheesecloth), tie the ends and hang it over a dish for an hour. Make sure the yoghurt isn't stirred or disturbed otherwise you will lose it through the muslin.

Toast the cardamom, fennel and coriander seeds, peppercorns and cloves in a dry frying pan (skillet) over a medium heat until fragrant. Remove from the heat, allow to cool, then place in a food processor. Add the dried onions and blitz to a powder. In a bowl, combine this spice powder with the yoghurt, green chillies, coriander and mustard oil and season with salt. Coat the venison in the spiced mixture, then cover and leave to marinate in the refrigerator for at least 12 hours or preferably overnight.

To make the artichoke crisps, pour the oil in a heavy-based saucepan, and heat until it is about 180°C (350°F). The oil is hot enough when a cube of bread sizzles when dropped into it. Carefully lower the sliced artichokes, one at a time, into the oil and cook for 1–2 minutes until light golden brown in colour. Remove with a slotted spoon, drain on kitchen paper and sprinkle with chaat masala and chilli powder, if using.

Cook the marinated venison in a heavy-based frying pan (skillet) over a medium to hight for about 5 minutes, turning every minute or so. Remove the venison from the grill, brush with melted butter and leave to rest for 8 minutes. Slice each piece of venison, arrange on a plate and serve with the artichoke crisps and pumpkin chutney.

SERVES 4

200 g (7 oz/scant 1 cup) Greek yoghurt
½ tablespoon green cardamom pods
1 tablespoon fennel seeds
1 tablespoon coriander seeds
1 tablespoon black peppercorns
½ tablespoon cloves
2 tablespoons dried crispy onions
4 green chillies, finely chopped
1 bunch of fresh coriander (cilantro), finely chopped
3 tablespoons mustard oil
sea salt
2 tablespoons melted butter
4 x 200 g (7 oz) venison rump steaks
100 g (3½ oz) Pumpkin Chutney (see page 208)

FOR THE ARTICHOKE CRISPS

1 litre (34 fl oz/4 cups) vegetable oil, for deep-frying
200 g (7 oz) Jerusalem artichokes (sunchokes), peeled and thinly sliced
a good pinch of chaat masala
1 tablespoon Kashmiri red chilli powder (optional)

PICKLED BEEF

Pickling meat is another example of the resourcefulness of Indian cooking. I urge you to try this recipe — it is a great way to preserve your meat and make it last longer. I love to serve this on freshly toasted mini chapattis topped with some grated paneer, pickled shallots and shredded coriander, as shown in the picture.

Cut the steak into 2 cm (¾ in) pieces. Wash in cold water 3 times, then sprinkle with a large pinch of salt to extract some of the moisture from the meat. Leave the meat draining in a colander for about 20 minutes.

Put the meat in a dry frying pan (skillet) and cook slowly, stirring continuously, to extract the moisture. Once all the moisture has evaporated, remove the meat from the pan.

Add the mustard and vegetable oils to the same pan, then, once hotm fry the beef, in batches, to colour. Once the meat is all cooked, turn the heat off. Add the ginger and garlic paste, chilli powder and turmeric to the pan, stir and leave to cool.

To store, place the beef pieces in a sterilised jar, pour the cooled flavoured oil on top, followed by the fenugreek, mustard, lime and malt vinegar and season with a little salt. Stir together so that all the flavours infuse.

Store at room temperature for up to a week.

SERVES 10

1 kg (2 lb 3 oz) bavette (flank) steak
a generous pinch of sea salt
200 ml (7 fl oz/scant 1 cup) mustard oil
200 ml (7 fl oz/scant 1 cup) vegetable oil
6 tablespoons Ginger & Garlic Paste
  (see page 183)
4 tablespoons Kashmiri red chilli powder
2 tablespoons ground turmeric
1 tablespoon ground fenugreek
1 tablespoon ground mustard seeds
200 ml (7 fl oz/scant 1 cup) lime juice
200 ml (7 fl oz/scant 1 cup) malt vinegar

OLD DELHI CHICKEN

The sauce that forms the base of this dish is derived from the classic old Delhi chicken (or, as we know it, butter chicken) recipe, originally created by a restaurant called Moti Mahal in old Delhi. It should be smooth, creamy, slightly spicy and flecked with the green of dried fenugreek leaves. When I first tried the sauce in Delhi it reminded me of a spicy version of Heinz tomato soup from a can (in a good way!) so don't be alarmed if you get the same flavour at the end of making the sauce!

First make the marinade. To hang the yoghurt, turn it out of its packaging straight into a muslin (cheesecloth), tie the ends and hang it over a dish for 1 hour. Make sure the yoghurt isn't stirred or disturbed otherwise you will lose it through the muslin.

Put the yoghurt in a bowl and add the marinade ingredients and stir together. Add the chicken to the bowl and coat in the marinade. Cover and leave in the refrigerator for 12 hours, or overnight.

When ready to make the sauce, heat the oil in a saucepan over a medium heat, add the whole spices and allow them to infuse in the oil for 30 seconds or so before adding the ginger and garlic paste, chilli powder and green chillies. Cook for a couple of minutes then turn the heat down to medium-low, add the tomatoes, then cover and cook for about 30 minutes until the sauce has reduced by one-third and the oil has separated from the tomatoes. Remove the whole spices, then add the cream, butter, garam masala and fenugreek leaves. Season to taste with sugar and salt. Let the sauce simmer as you cook the chicken.

Sear the marinated thighs in a hot pan for about 15 minutes until just cooked through, then add them to the sauce. Mix and adjust the seasoning, if required. Just before serving, drizzle with some cream and top with fresh coriander and ginger.

SERVES 4

8 boneless, skinless, free-range chicken thighs, cut into 2.5 cm (1 in) pieces
a handful of micro coriander (cilantro) cress
1 thumb-size piece of fresh ginger root, very finely sliced into strips

FOR THE MARINADE

300 g (10½ oz/1¼ cups) Greek yoghurt
3 tablespoons mustard oil
2 tablespoons Ginger & Garlic Paste (see page 183)
1 tablespoon ground turmeric
1 tablespoon Kashmiri red chilli powder
2 teaspoons sea salt

FOR THE SAUCE

2 tablespoons vegetable oil
4 green cardamom pods
2 black cardamom pods
4 cloves
2 fresh Indian bay leaves
4 tablespoons Ginger & Garlic Paste (see page 183)
2 tablespoons red Kashmiri red chilli powder
2 green chillies, split down the middle
1 kg (2 lb 3 oz) plum tomatoes, puréed
200 ml (7 fl oz/scant 1 cup) double (heavy) cream, plus extra to serve
250 g (9 oz/1 cup) unsalted butter
1 tablespoon garam masala
a handful of dried fenugreek leaves
caster (superfine) sugar, to taste
sea salt, to taste
6 tablespoons mustard oil

DUCK LEG KATHI ROLL WITH PEANUT CHUTNEY & PICKLED CUCUMBER

This is our interpretation of the famous kathi roll from Calcutta, usually made using chicken, egg or vegetables. Here we use duck meat, which pairs perfectly with the peanut chutney and pickled cucumber. You can find frozen Malabar parathas in any good Indian store.

To make the spice mix, first, roast the cloves, cumin and star anise over a high heat in a dry frying pan (skillet) for 30 seconds or so until fragrant and lightly browned. Allow to cool, then place in a blender and blitz to a powder.

Mix the spice blend with the minced duck in a bowl, then add the green chillies, ginger and garlic paste, chilli powder, coriander and garam masala and salt. Fold in the red onion. Divide into 6 balls and make into sausage shapes, then cover and leave to rest in the refrigerator until needed.

Heat the oil in a large frying pan and cook the duck kebabs for about 10 minutes, turning them frequently, until cooked through and nicely browned.

At the same time, finish cooking the parathas on a hot *tawa* or dry frying pan, until golden brown. Brush each of the parathas with coriander chutney, then add a cooked kebab, peanut chutney and pickled cucumber. Make a roll, cutting off the edges and serve while still warm.

SERVES 6

1 kg (2 lb 3 oz) duck leg meat, minced (ground)
1 tablespoon vegetable oil
4–6 ready-made Malabar parathas
4 teaspoons Coriander Chutney (see page 195), to serve
Peanut Chutney (see page 196), to serve
150 g (5 oz) Pickled Cucumber (see page 92), to serve

FOR THE SPICE MIX

5 cloves
1 teaspoon ground cumin
3 star anise
4 green chillies, finely chopped
3 Ginger & Garlic Paste (see page 183)
1 tablespoon Kashmiri red chilli powder
3 tablespoons coriander stalks, finely chopped
2 tablespoons garam masala
2 teaspoons sea salt
1 large red onion, finely chopped

111

BLACK STONE FLOWER LAMB CHOPS WITH BURNT ONION RAITA

The marinade for the lamb in this recipe is fairly complex, but the result is wonderfully fragrant. If you can, prepare the chops the night before, so that the meat has plenty of time to marinate. I love to serve them a squeeze of lemon juice for extra zing.

Begin by making the spice mix for the lamb chops. Gently toast the allspice, cloves, cumin, cinnamon and peppercorns in a dry pan for a few minutes or so until fragrant and lightly toasted. Allow to cool, then place in a food processor and blitz to a powder.

Place the lamb chops in a bowl, with the powdered spice mix, oil, ginger and garlic paste, turmeric, lemon juice, green chilli, mint, onion paste and salt. Using your hands, coat the meat in the marinade then cover and leave in the refrigerator until needed, preferably overnight.

Half an hour before cooking the marinated chops, take them out of the refrigerator to bring up to room temperature. Heat a heavy-based frying pan (skillet) over a high heat, and cook the chops, turning them occasionally, for about 8 minutes until the outside is charred but the meat is tender and slightly pink inside. Alternatively, you can also cook them on a very hot barbecue or griddle pan.

Brush the chops with butter, dress with a squeeze of lemon and a pinch of chaat masala, and allow to rest for 10 minutes before serving with the burnt onion raita and wild garlic chutney. Drizzle over any of the leftover juices from the pan.

SERVES 4

8 lamb chops
2 tablespoons vegetable oil
3 tablespoons Ginger & Garlic Paste (see page 183)
1 tablespoon ground turmeric
100 ml (3½ fl oz/scant ½ cup) lemon juice
3 green chillies, finely chopped
3 tablespoons finely chopped fresh mint leaves
2 tablespoons store-bought green papaya paste (optional)
1 small onion, minced to a paste
2 teaspoon sea salt
a knob of unsalted butter, melted
a squeeze of lemon juice
a pinch of chaat masala
200 g (7 oz) Burnt Onion Raita (see page 216), to serve
Wild Garlic Chutney (see page 203), to serve

FOR THE SPICE MIX

1 teaspoon ground allspice
½ teaspoon ground cloves
1 teaspoon ground cumin
1 cinnamon stick
1 teaspoon black peppercorns

LAMB HALEEM WITH FRESH GINGER

Made with four different grains, this is essentially a lamb porridge, but don't let that put you off! It's perfect winter comfort food and hails from Hyderabad, where the dish made its name. Serve with a steaming bowl of rice and lightly buttered chapatis.

Heat the oil in a frying pan (skillet) over a medium to high heat, and fry the lamb pieces with the wholes spices for a few minutes or so until lightly coloured. Add 4 tablespoons of the ginger and garlic paste, season with salt, cover and cook over a low to medium heat for about 1 hour until the lamb is tender.

Put the wheat and dals in a large saucepan, cover with water, bring to the boil then cover and simmer for about 40 minutes until they are completely cooked and all the water has been absorbed. Using a stick blender, blitz the mixture until smooth.

Heat the ghee in a large, deep saucepan. Add the remaining ginger and garlic paste, the ground coriander, chilli powder, turmeric and chillies. Mix in the cooked lamb and stir for a few minutes. Reserve a little of the fresh coriander and mint for garnish and add the remainder to the saucepan with the garam masala. Adjust the seasoning as necessary and serve garnished with the fried onions, and reserved coriander, mint. For added texture sprinkle over some puffed wheat.

SERVES 8

1 tablespoon vegetable oil
500 g (1 lb 2 oz) lamb shoulder, cut into
    2.5 cm (1 in) pieces
500 g (1 lb 2 oz) lamb leg, cut into
    2.5 cm (1 in) pieces
2 green cardamom pods
1 black cardamom pod
½ teaspoon cloves
2 fresh Indian bay leaves
8 tablespoons Ginger & Garlic Paste (see page 183)
2 teaspoons sea salt
100 g (3½ oz) wheat grains
2 tablespoons yellow moong dal (lentils), washed
2 tablespoons channa dal (lentils), washed
2 tablespoons urad dal (lentils), washed
100 g (3½ oz) ghee
300 g (10½ oz) onions, fried
1 tablespoon ground coriander
1 tablespoon Kashmiri red chilli powder
1 tablespoon ground turmeric
4 green chillies, finely chopped
1 bunch of fresh coriander, chopped
1 bunch of fresh mint leaves, finely julienned
1 tablespoon garam masala
a handful of puffed wheat, to garnish

GUINEA FOWL MAPPAS WITH SALLI POTATOES

Salli potatoes are like very thin matchstick chips (see recipe photo on page 123). They have their origins in Middle Eastern cooking and they adorn many Parsi dishes. Parsis are Indians of Iranian descent and you will still find several Parsi cafés in Mumbai. Britannia & Co. in Fort, South Mumbai, is perhaps the oldest and most famous. Their food is delicious and their family recipes are closely guarded by the owner, Mr Kohinoor.

To cook the salli potatoes, pour the oil in a heavy-based saucepan or *kadai*, and heat until it is about 180°C (350°F). The oil is hot enough when a cube of bread sizzles when dropped into it. Add the potatoes and fry for about 10 minutes until golden brown. Remove from the oil using a slotted spoon and drain on kitchen paper. Season with chaat masala. Leave in a warm place until needed.

To make the sauce, heat the oil in a large saucepan, add the mustard seeds and fry for 30 seconds or so until they splutter, then add the curry leaves then the onions. Cook over a medium heat for about 10 minutes until the onions start to turn translucent. Add the ginger and garlic paste, the green chillies and chopped ginger and cook for another 2 minutes. Then add the guinea fowl pieces and cook for a few minutes, stirring occasionally to allow the meat to take on a little colour.

Add the coconut milk, bring to the boil then turn the heat down to a simmer and cook for about 20 minutes until the guinea fowl pieces are tender.

Once the meat is cooked, add ground coriander, garam masala and white wine vinegar and season to taste with salt. Serve the guinea fowl in its sauce, garnished generously with the salli potatoes.

SERVES 4

2 whole guinea fowl, quartered

FOR THE SALLI POTATOES

1 litre (34 fl oz/4 cups) vegetable oil, for deep-frying
1 large Maris Piper potato, peeled and julienned
a pinch of chaat masala

FOR THE SAUCE

1 tablespoon vegetable oil
1 tablespoon mustard seeds
a handful of fresh curry leaves
2 brown onions, thinly sliced
2 tablespoons Ginger & Garlic Paste (see page 183)
2 whole green chillies, slit in half
a thumb-size piece of fresh ginger root, peeled and finely chopped
500 ml (17 fl oz/2 cups) coconut milk
2 tablespoons ground coriander
2 tablespoons garam masala
3 tablespoons distilled white vinegar
sea salt

WILD
BOAR
LAAL MAAS

Laal maas is a traditional hunter dish that would be prepared in advance and would keep for days due to the amount of spices, salt and ghee in the dish. Traditionally, wild game was used in the dish but since there was a ban put on any game hunting in India, goat is now preferred. We want to take the dish back to its roots by using wild boar. If you can't get hold of wild boar, venison will also work really well.

Heat 300 g (10½ oz) of the ghee in a large frying pan (skillet) over a medium heat, add the whole spices, then the onions and cook for about 10 minutes until golden brown.

Add the boar pieces and cook over a medium heat for a few minutes, stirring occasionally until browned. Stir in the ginger and garlic paste, chutney, chilli powder, mango powder, if using, yoghurt and cumin, mix thoroughly, cover and cook over a low to medium heat for at least an hour until the boar is tender. Add a little water if you feel the mixture is getting too dry.

Once the meat is cooked, season to taste with salt. Remove from the heat and garnish with fresh coriander.

When ready to serve, heat up the charcoal until it is grey, place in the middle of the pan, pour the remaining ghee onto the charcoal and you will see it immediately smoke. Serve at once.

SERVES 4

400 g (14 oz) ghee
4 green cardamom pods
2 black cardamom pods
3 blades of mace
3 fresh Indian bay leaves
1 teaspoon cloves
2 cinnamon sticks
3 onions, thinly sliced
500 g (1 lb 2 oz) boneless wild boar shoulder,
    cut into 2.5 cm (1 in) pieces
2 tablespoons Ginger & Garlic Paste (see page 183)
2 tablespoons Chilli Garlic chutney (188)
1 tablespoon Kashmiri red chilli powder
2 teaspoons green mango powder, optional
400 g (14 oz/1⅔ cups) Greek yoghurt
2 tablespoons ground cumin
sea salt, to taste
1 bunch of fresh coriander (cilantro),
    finely chopped
1 small piece of charcoal

GROUSE & COCO BEAN MASALA WITH COBNUT CRUMBLE

Grouse, and other dark game birds, pair very well with Indian spices. Here we marinate the meat and serve it pink, as shown in the photograph. The flavour of the cloves is quite strong, so don't add more than needed as it can overpower the flavour of the meat.

To make the spice mix, toast the peppercorns, bay leaves cinnamon and cardamom pods in a dry frying pan (skillet) for a few minutes until fragrant. Leave to cool, then place into a food procressor and blitz to form a fine powder.

Combining the spice mix with the ginger and garlic paste, vegetable oil, chilli powder and salt. Add the grouse breasts, coat in them in the marinade, cover and set aside in the refrigerator to marinate, ideally overnight.

For the coco bean masala, heat the oil in a saucepan over a medium heat, and fry the whole spices for a minute or so. Add the ginger and garlic paste and continue to cook for a couple minutes then add the chillies, onions and tomatoes and simmer for about 15 minutes until the sauce has reduced by half.

Add the coco beans with the cumin, coriander and turmeric, and season to taste with sugar and salt. Add a little water, cover and cook for 30 minutes until the beans have absorbed the flavours and moisture from the sauce. Remove from the heat and season with the channa masala spice mix.

For the cobnut crumble, place the toasted cobnuts and sesame seeds with the remaining ingredients, in a blender and pulse to a crumble.

Cook the marinated grouse in a frying pan over a high heat, for about 3 minutes each side for medium rare, then rest for 6 minutes. Slice and serve on top of the coco bean masala, garnish with the coriander cress and serve with the pickled red onions and cobnut crumble.

SERVES 4

4 whole grouse, breasts removed from the bone
fresh coriander (cilantro) cress, to serve
Pickled Red Onions (see page 133), to serve

FOR THE SPICE MIX

1 teaspoon black peppercorns
2 Indian bay leaf
1 cinnamon stick
½ teaspoon green cardamom pods
2 tablespoons Ginger & Garlic Paste (see page 183)
3 tablespoons vegetable oil
1 teaspoon red Kashmiri red chilli powder
2 teaspoons sea salt

FOR THE COCO BEAN MASALA

1 tablespoon vegetable oil
2 Indian bay leaves
1 cinnamon stick
1 teaspoon peppercorns
¼ teaspoon cardamom pods
2 tablespoons Ginger & Garlic Paste (see page 183)
2 green chillies, finely chopped
2 large red onions, puréed
500 g (1 lb 2 oz) tomatoes, puréed
500 g (1 lb 2 oz) fresh coco or haricot beans
1 tablespoon ground cumin
1 tablespoon ground coriander
½ tablespoon ground turmeric
caster (superfine) sugar, to taste
sea salt, to taste
1 tablespoon channa masala spice mix

FOR THE COBNUT CRUMBLE

100 g (3½ oz/¾ cup) cobnuts or hazelnuts, toasted
50 g (2 oz/⅓ cup) sesame seeds, toasted
1 teaspoon Kashmiri red chilli powder
1 teaspoon chaat masala

KID OFFAL KEEMA

If you can find kid offal, adding the liver and kidneys to an otherwise traditional keema adds depth and richness to the dish and gives it an almost silky quality. If you can't get hold of it, lamb offal or any other available type will work well.

In a deep heavy-based saucepan, heat the ghee and fry the whole spices for a few minutes or so until fragrant and lightly toasted. Add the onions and the ginger and garlic paste and cook for about 10 minutes until caramelised.

Add all the meat to the pan and stir continuously over a high heat for about 10 minutes until nicely browned. Add the chilli, cumin, turmeric and coriander and cook for a further 2 minutes before adding tomatoes. Cover and let it simmer for a few minutes. Reduce the heat and cook the mixture over a medium heat for about 30–40 minutes until the meat has absorbed the flavours in the pan and the liquid of the tomatoes has all but gone. By this stage the meat should be cooked. Remove from the heat then add the yoghurt, ginger, dried fenugreek and garam masala. Season to taste with salt.

Meanwhile, make the sali potatoes according to the instructions on page 116. Set aside until ready to serve.

To serve, spoon into 4 bowls, top with watercress and a sprinkling of salli potatoes.

SERVES 4

100 g (3½ oz) ghee
½ tablespoon black peppercorns
½ tablespoon cloves
1 tablespoon cumin seeds
1 cinnamon stick
2 black cardamom pods
2 brown onions, finely chopped
3 tablespoons Ginger & Garlic Paste
  (see page 183)
250 g (9 oz) kid goat, minced (ground)
80 g (3 oz) venison liver
80 g (3 oz) kidneys, trimmed
1 tablespoon Kashmiri red chilli powder
1 tablespoon ground cumin
1 tablespoon ground turmeric
1 tablespoon ground coriander
500 g (1 lb 2 oz) plum tomatoes, puréed
200 g (7 oz/scant 1 cup) Greek yoghurt
80 g (3 oz) fresh ginger root, peeled
  and julienned
2 tablespoons dried fenugreek leaves
1 tablespoon garam masala
sea salt, to taste
a sprinking of Salli Potatoes (see page 116)
1 bunch of fresh watercress

VEGETABLES

When I was a child, I loved vegetables. I wasn't the picky infant who pushed aside broccoli, sprouts and carrots and would only eat frozen peas – I ate everything on offer! So when I went to India, I was inspired and excited by the range and variety of vegetables. As the majority of Indians are vegetarian, they have learnt to cook their produce in so many inventive and inspiring ways. Vegetables are shredded, sliced, stir-fried, pickled, steamed, and infused to become the stars of the show.

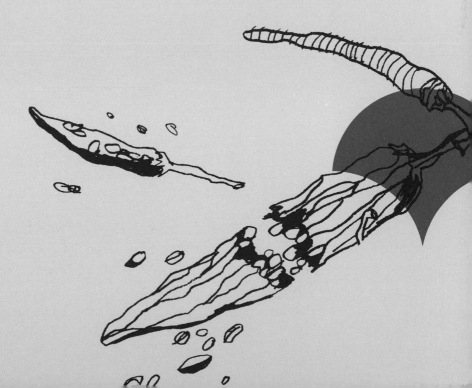

BHEL
PURI

This is another signature Kricket dish that has been on the menu since day one. Each street vendor in Mumbai has their own version – perhaps just changing a few spices – and we have kept this recipe fairly traditional. The only aspect that you wouldn't typically see is the addition of yoghurt, which I believe is needed to balance the moisture levels in the dish. It's incredibly quick to make and virtually all raw so it's healthy to boot! You will find both bhel mix and sev in most Indian stores. Bhel mix is made from puffed rice and vegetables while sev is a deep-fried chickpea-noodle snack seasoned with turmeric.

Beat the yoghurt in a bowl and sweeten to taste with sugar. Set aside until ready to serve.

Put the bhel mix in a bowl, add the onion and mango, along with the coriander chutney and chaat masala. Mix well.

Spoon the mixture into mounds on 4 serving plates, then generously spoon over the yoghurt and tamarind and date chutney, leaving some yoghurt visible. Sprinkle the sev, and top with the fresh coriander.

Serve immediately as will become soggy very quickly.

SERVES 4

4 tablespoons yoghurt
caster (superfine) sugar, to taste
100 g (3½ oz) store-bought bhel mix
½ red onion, finely diced
1 green raw mango, finely diced
4 tablespoons Coriander Chutney (see page 195)
4 pinches of chaat masala
4 tablespoons Tamarind & Date Chutney
  (see page 184)
80 g (3 oz) store-bought sev
a small handful of coriander (cilantro) cress
  or finely chopped coriander leaves

JERSEY ROYAL ALOO CHAAT

Lotus root and sev adds real texture and bite to this dish. You shoud be able to find both of these ingredients at your local Indian store. Ramsons are the flowers of wild garlic leaves that grow in the woodlands during Spring. Fermenting is a great way to preserve this special ingredient, making it available all year round: simply sprinkle the whole ramson flower heads with a little sea salt. Massage the salt into the ramsons for around 10 minutes then pound them using a rolling pin to break down the plant fibres and release more liquid. Transfer the ramsons to a flat tray — you will start to see the moisture come out of the flowers. Pour the plant matter and all it's liquid into a sterilised jar, and press it down to make sure it's completely submerged in it's liquid. Leave for 2–3 weeks before tasting. This dish also works well with the Wild Garlic Chutney on page 203.

Cook the potatoes in a pan of boiling salted water for about 15 minutes until just tender. Drain and leave to cool. Crush the potatoes gently with your hand just to break the skins.

Pour the oil in a heavy-based saucepan, and heat until it is about 180°C (350°F). The oil is hot enough when a cube of bread sizzles when dropped into it.

Deep-fry the potatoes for about 5 minutes until crisp and golden. Remove from the pan, drain on kitchen paper, then season with chaat masala.

Put the chickpeas in a bowl along with with the coriander chutney, red onion, one-third of the tamarind chutney, one-third of the sweetened yogurt and half the coriander. Season well to taste with salt and chaat masala. Mix the chickpeas with the potatoes, then spoon into 4 serving bowls. Top with the remaining tamarind chutney, yoghurt and coriander, the sev, pomegranate seeds, ramsons and lotus root crisps. Serve immediately.

SERVES 4

400 g (14 oz) Jersey royal potatoes, washed and cut in half

1 litre (34 fl oz/4 cups) vegetable oil, for deep-frying

4 generous pinches of chaat masala, plus extra for seasoning

200 g (7 oz/scant 1½ cups) canned chickpeas (garbanzos), drained and rinsed

4 tablespoons Coriander Chutney (see page 195)

1 large red onion, finely chopped

5 tablespoons Tamarind & Date Chutney (see page 184)

5 tablespoons sweetened Greek yoghurt

a handful of fresh coriander (cilantro), finely chopped

sea salt, to taste

a handful of sev

1 small pomegranate, halved and seeds scooped out

3 tablespoons fermented ramsons (see recipe introduction, above)

1 lotus root, thinly fried until crisp

DAL MAKHANI

The ultimate comfort food. In India, I used to walk into the restaurant every morning to the sight of a huge pot of these lentils cooking over the continuous heat of the tandoor. Done right, they are perfect on their own, or they can be served with chapatis or as a side dish with pretty much any of the main dishes in this book.

Soak the dal in a bowl of water for 2 hours, or overnight if possible.

Drain the dal, then place in a saucepan with half the onions, the green chillies and half the asafoetida and season with salt. Add 1.5 litres (52 fl oz/6½ cups) water and bring to the boil, then cook for 30–40 minutes until the dal has completely disintegrated and smooth. Add more water if it dries out during cooking.

In a separate pan, heat the oil and add the cumin seeds and the remaining asafoetida. Stir for 30 seconds or so until the seeds start to crackle, then add the remaining onions and fry for about 10 minutes over a medium heat until golden.

Add the ginger and garlic paste and fry for a minute before adding the tomatoes, coriander, cumin and chilli powder. Season to taste with salt.

Add the boiled dal to the tomato spice mixture plus enough additional water (if required). You should end up with a thick, smooth consistency. Simmer, with the lid on, for 5–10 minutes, stirring througout. Pour in the cream, butter and ghee and mix well. Remove from the heat, check the seasoning and serve straight away.

SERVES 4

500 g (1 lb 2 oz) urad dal (lentils), washed
4 onions, chopped or sliced
3 green chillies, whole or chopped
1 teaspoon asafoetida
sea salt, to taste
1 tablespoon vegetable oil
1 tablespoon cumin seeds
2 tablespoons Ginger & Garlic Paste (see page 183)
200 g (7 oz) tomatoes, chopped
2 tablespoons ground coriander
2 tablespoons ground cumin
2 tablespoons Kashmiri red chilli powder
200 ml (7 fl oz/scant 1 cup) double (heavy) cream
3 tablespoons unsalted butter
2 tablespoons ghee

CHOLE BATURA

When I was motor biking around Leh Ladakh, in India, it was low season, which meant that many of the local restaurants were shut. And the only dishes I could find on the side of the roads were Punjabi samosas and chole batura. Despite the sun, the temperatures were low and chole was the perfect remedy to this. It's all I ate — I couldn't get enough of it!

First make the dough for the batura. Put the flour into mixing bowl with a pinch of salt and the vegetable oil. Gradually add enough water to form a stiff dough. Cover and set aside to rest until needed.

To make the pickled red onions, steep the onions in the pickling liquor for 1–2 hours at room temperature, then keep in the refrigerator until needed.

For the chole, heat the oil in a heavy-based saucepan over a medium heat, and fry the whole spices for 30 seconds or so, until they start to splutter. Add the tomatoes and the ginger and garlic paste, and simmer for about 15 minutes until the sauce has reduced by a third and is thick in consistency. Add the ground spices and the chickpeas and cook over a low heat until the chickpeas have absorbed most of the liquid from the tomatoes. This should take around 30 minutes. Add the channa masala and season to taste.

Heat a deep frying pan (skillet) or *kadai* with a little oil (about 2 in/5 cm). Shallow-fry the batura for about 4 minutes on each side until puffed up and lightly browned. Drain on kitchen paper then serve alongside the the chole and pickled red onions.

SERVES 4

2 tablespoons vegetable oil, plus extra for frying
2 green chillies, finely chopped
2 fresh Indian bay leaves
1 cinnamon stick
1 teaspoon black peppercorns, crushed
4 green cardamom pods
800 g (2 lb 12 oz) tomatoes, puréed
2 tablespoons Ginger & Garlic Paste
  (see page 183)
1 tablespoon ground cumin
1 tablespoon ground coriander
½ tablespoon ground turmeric
400 g (14 oz/2¾ cups) tin chickpeas
  (garbanzos), drained and rinsed
2 tablespoons channa masala spice mix
sea salt, to taste

FOR THE BATURA

200 g (7 oz/1½ cups) wholewheat flour
a pinch of salt
2½ tablespoons vegetable oil
approx. 100 ml (3½ fl oz) cold filtered water,
  plus more if required

FOR THE PICKLED RED ONIONS

2 red onions, thinly sliced
200 ml (7 fl oz/scant 1 cup) Pickling Liquor
  (see page 183)

HYDERABAD BABY AUBERGINE WITH COCONUT & CURRY LEAF

This is a dish common to Hyderabad. It has a lovely creamy texture with a spicy, slightly nutty taste. I love to serve this with a sprinkling of fried onions as pictured, but you can also top it with freshly grated coconut.

Prepare the aubergines by making a deep cross with a knife at the base of each one. Soak them in heavily salted water for 30 minutes, then drain. The salt water will extract any excess water within the aubergine.

Heat 1 tablespoon of the oil in a large frying pan (skillet) and fry the aubergines for about 5 minutes until just cooked. Drain and set aside to be added to the masala later.

Wipe the oil residue from the pan and dry-toast the desiccated coconut, peanuts, sesame, coriander and cumin seeds for 30 seconds or so until fragrant. Leave to cool, then blitz in a food processor with the green chillies, fresh coriander and a little water, if necessary, to form a paste.

Heat the remaining oil in the same pan, over a medium heat, add the mustard seeds and curry leaves and fry for 30 seconds or so until they start to splutter, then add the onions and cook for 10 minutes until translucent. Add the ginger and garlic paste, turmeric and chilli powder, followed by the coconut milk. Bring to the boil, then turn down to a simmer, cover and cook for around 20 minutes until everything is soft and well blended. Season to taste with salt and the tamarind chutney.

Add the aubergines to the sauce and cook for a further 10 minutes. Just before serving, garnish with the fried onions and a few fried curry leaves.

SERVES 4

8 baby aubergines (eggplants)
sea salt, to taste
a sprinkle of fried onions, to garnish
a few fried curry leaves, to garnish

FOR THE MASALA

2 tablespoons vegetable oil
100 g (3½ oz/generous 1 cup) desiccated
  (dried shredded) coconut
50 g (2 oz/⅓ cup) unsalted peanuts
40 g (1½ oz/¼ cup) white sesame seeds
4 teaspoons coriander seeds
4 teaspoons cumin seeds
2 green chillies
1 small bunch of fresh coriander
1 teaspoon black mustard seeds
80 g (3 oz) packet of fresh curry leaves
2 brown onions, finely chopped
2 tablespoons Ginger & Garlic Paste (see page 183)
1 teaspoon ground turmeric
1 tablespoon Kashmiri red chilli powder
500 ml (17 fl oz/2 cups) coconut milk
sea salt, to taste
100 ml (3½ fl oz/scant ½ cup) Tamarind & Date
  Chutney (see page 186)

DELICA PUMPKIN WITH MAKHANI SAUCE & HAZELNUT CRUMBLE

One of the most popular dishes on our menu, and one that will stay on for a while! The sauce is the original butter chicken sauce that I tried in a restaurant in old Delhi, called Moti Mahal. Delica pumpkins are quite small and have a much sweeter flesh than a regular pumpkin. They have a relatively short season. You can buy them from any good grocer in season but if they are not available, just use another pumpkin variety instead or butternut squash.

Preheat the oven to 160ºC (320ºF/Gas 3).

Halve the pumpkin, scoop out the seeds, slice the flesh into 8 wedges and trim the ends. Put the pumpkin slices in a roasting pan and coat with the oil, cumin, turmeric, chilli powder and salt. Roast in the oven for around 30 minutes. You want the pumpkin to be only just cooked, as it gets a further grilling (broiling) before being served.

While it is roasting, make the puffed rice. Heat a little oil, to about 2 cm (1 in) in depth, in a heavy-based saucepan until very hot. Add the wild rice and stir for a few minutes until it puffs up, then drain on kitchen paper.

To make the hazelnut crumble, toast the nuts and sesame seeds with the chilli powder for a few minutes until golden in a dry frying pan (skillet). Cool, then roughly pulse to a fine powder, in a food procressor, with the chaat masala.

Heat up the makhani sauce and spoon into 4 plates or bowls. Grill (broil) the pumpkin for a few minutes on each side, until the slices get a little colour – this will add a smoky element to the dish.

To serve, arrange 2 wedges of pumpkin on top of the sauce, and top with the crumbled paneer, hazelnut crumble, puffed wild rice and garnish with coriander.

SERVES 4

1 Delica pumpkin, about 18 cm (7 in)
   in diameter
1 teaspoon vegetable oil, plus extra for frying
1 teaspoon ground cumin
1 teaspoon ground turmeric
1 teaspoon Kashmiri red chilli powder
a generous pinch of sea salt
100 g (3½ oz/½ cup) wild rice
1 recipe quantity of Makhani Sauce
   from Old Delhi Chicken Sauce (see page 108)
200 g (7 oz) Paneer (see page 213), crumbled
a bunch of fresh micro coriander (cilantro),
   to garnish

FOR THE HAZELNUT CRUMBLE

200 g (7 oz/1½ cups) hazelnuts
50 g (2 oz/⅓ cup) sesame seeds
2 teaspoons Kashmiri red chilli powder
1 teaspoon chaat masala

VEGETABLES

SAMPHIRE PAKORAS WITH TAMARIND & DATE CHUTNEY

The original samphire pakora – on our menu since day one – makes the perfect snack. The whole dish is sweet, salty, sour and spicy, and is incredibly moreish!

Mix together the chickpea flour, chilli powder and turmeric, then gradually whisk in about 150–200 ml (5–7 fl oz/¾–scant 1 cup) water to create a thick pancake-style batter. Evenly coat the samphire in the batter.

Pour the oil in a heavy-based saucepan or *kadai*, and heat until it is about 180°C (350°F). The oil is hot enough when a cube of bread sizzles when dropped into it.

Drop in the battered samphire in spoonfuls, moving it constantly within the pan to ensure it doesn't stick together, and fry for a few minutes. Once golden brown and crispy, lift the samphire out of the oil with a slotted spoon and drain on kitchen paper. Season with sugar and very little salt, then serve with the tamarind and date chutney and chilli garlic mayonnaise on the side.

SERVES 4

150 g (5 oz/1⅓ cups) chickpea (gram) flour
2 teaspoons Kashmiri red chilli powder
1½ teaspoon ground turmeric
300 g (10½ oz) samphire
1 litre (34 fl oz/4 cups) vegetable oil,
  for deep-frying
caster (superfine) sugar, to taste
sea salt, to taste
Tamarind & Date Chutney (see page 184)
Chilli Garlic Mayonnaise (see page 187)

SMOKED AUBERGINE WITH SESAME RAITA & PAPDI GATHYA

Usually we cook the aubergine (eggplant) for this dish on a skewer in the tandoor. The smoke from the coals helps add the smoky flavour to the aubergine when it is cooking. If you don't have a tandoor, cook them in the oven instead, and the results will be nearly as good. Alternatively, use a grill (brioler) or a barbecue and that should help you achieve the smoky flavour. You can find papdi gathya in most Indian stores.

Preheat the oven to 160°C (320°F/Gas 3).

Drizzle the aubergines with a little oil, then place on a baking tray and cook in the oven for 30 minutes until soft and the skin has charred. Alternatively, you can cook them under a hot grill (brioler). Check that they are completely soft, then remove from the oven. (Keep the oven on as you'll need it later for the peanut crumble.) While the aubergies are still warm, put them in a large bowl, cover with cling film (plastic wrap) and leave for 10 minutes to cool. Peel off the skin and blitz the flesh into a rough paste in a blender.

Heat the oil in a large pan with the mustard and cumin seeds, half of the curry leaves, the green chillies, ginger and garlic paste, turmeric and chilli powder. Remove from the heat and stir through the aubergine, then add the remaining ingredients. Season to taste with sugar and salt.

To make the peanut crumble, put the nuts in a roasting pan and roast in the oven for about 10 minutes. Add the remaining ingredients and cook for a further 5 minutes. Allow to cool before roughly blitzing in a food procressor.

Just before serving, garnish the aubergine with the coriander, pomegranate seeds and peanut crumble and serve with a spoon of sesame raita and some gathya to scoop up the dish.

SERVES 4

8 large aubergines (eggplants)
100 ml (3½ fl oz/scant ½ cup) vegetable oil, plus 1 tablespoon to drizzle over the aubergines
1 teaspoon black mustard seeds
2 teaspoons cumin seeds
80 g (3 oz) fresh curry leaves
3 green chillies, finely chopped
1 tablespoon Ginger & Garlic Paste (see page 183)
1 tablespoon turmeric
2 teaspoons Kashmiri red chilli powder
a large handful of fresh coriander (cilantro), finely chopped
1 tablespoon garam masala
1 teaspoon ground mustard seed
1 teaspoon ground fenugreek
a squeeze of lemon juice
2 red onions, finely chopped and sprinkled with salt, then squeezed to remove excess moisture
sugar, to taste
sea salt, to taste

FOR THE PEANUT CRUMBLE

100 g (3½ oz) roasted unsalted peanuts
50 g (2 oz) sesame seeds
1 teaspoon Kashmiri red chilli powder
½ teaspoon chaat masala

TO GARNISH

1 small bunch of coriander (cilantro) cress
200 g (7 oz) Sesame Raita (see page 205)
200g (7oz) papdi gathya
seeds of 1 small pomegranate

BURNT GARLIC
TARKA DAL

This dish is completely unadulterated; the tradtional method is so easy and the dish is delicious enough as it is, so I didn't want to mess with it! It is the perfect comfort food that can be served with rice or paratha or eaten on its own, like a soup.

Soak the dal in water for 20 minutes. Rinse and drain, then put in a saucepan and cover with 800 ml (28 fl oz/3½ cups) water, bring to the boil, then simmer for at least 40 minutes until the dal has absorbed all the liquid and has completely cooked. Add more water if the dal is drying out during the cooking process. It should be a thick, semi-smooth consistency.

In a separate saucepan, heat the oil, add the dried chillies and fry for a few seconds for the chillies to infuse in the oil. Add the garlic and fry to just before the point of burning. Add the shallots, ginger, cumin seeds, green chillies, curry leaves and the tomatoes.

Stir continuously over a high heat until thoroughly hot and blended before turning it all into the dal. Season to taste with salt, stir to combine and serve hot as it is, or with chapatis or plain basmati rice.

SERVES 4

500 g (1 lb 2 oz/2 cups) yellow moong dal, (lentils) washed
1 tablespoon vegetable oil
2 dried Kashmiri red chilli
5 garlic cloves, peeled and minced
2 banana shallots, finely chopped
a thumb-size piece of fresh ginger root, finely chopped
1 tablespoon cumin seeds
2 green chillies, split
80 g (3 oz) fresh curry leaves
2 tomatoes, roughly chopped
sea salt, to taste
Chapatis (see page 28) or plain rice, to serve

CHANTERELLES IN MALAI SAUCE WITH FRESH PEAS & PEA SHOOTS

This dish should be made in the autumn when chanterelles are at their best. The sauce is light and only slightly spiced to make sure that the flavour of the mushrooms shine.

Drain the soaked cashew nuts, then blend them with the water in a food procrressor to form a paste.

In a deep saucepan, heat up the oil over a low heat, then add the ginger and garlic paste, green chillies and onions and cook, stirring continuously, until the water has evaporated from the onions. Add the cashew nut paste and garam masala and cook for a further 10 minutes.

Add the mango, fenugreek leaves and cream and cook for a further 5 minutes until all the ingredients are soft and well blended. Remove from the heat then blitz with a hand blender to give it a smoother consistency.

Heat 4 tablespoons of water in a saucepan, add the butter and stir until melted, then add the mushrooms and cook for about 10 minutes until the mushrooms are soft. Add the peas and season to taste with a little salt plus a squeeze of lemon. Serve the sauce topped with the mushrooms and peas, and garnish with the pea shoots.

SERVES 4

200 g (7 oz/1¼ cups) unsalted cashew nuts,
   soaked in water for a few hours
200 ml (7 fl oz) water
1 tablespoon vegetable oil
2 tablespoons Ginger & Garlic Paste (see page 185)
2 green chillies, halved
2 brown onions, puréed
1 tablespoon garam masala
1 small green unripe mango, peeled, destoned
   and flesh finely chopped
a handful of fresh fenugreek leaves
200 ml (7 fl oz/scant 1 cup) double
   (heavy) cream
200 g (7 oz/scant 1 cup) unsalted butter
500 g (1 lb 2 oz) chanterelle (girolle) mushrooms
200 g (7 oz/1⅓ cups) fresh peas
sea salt, to taste
a squeeze of lemon juice
a handful of pea shoots, for garnish

147

GRILLED HISPI WITH CHILLI GARLIC CHUTNEY

This dish is perfect in the summer, cooked outside, on a barbecue for an intense, smoky flavour, and served alongside a selection of grilled fish or meat.

Season the cabbage with oil, cumin seeds and salt.

Grill (broil) the cabbage under a medium heat, for about 10 minutes, turning it every 2 minutes, until the centre of the cabbage is cooked and it is evenly charred. Alternatively, you can cook the cabbage in a griddle pan, over a high heat – just place the cabbage cut-side down and place a heavy plate on top, to ensure the cabbage is evenly charred.

Remove from the grill, drizzle with some chilli garlic chutney and a scattering of peanuts and serve with the sesame raita.

SERVES 4

2 hispi cabbage, cut into quarters
1 tablespoon vegetable oil
1 tablespoon cumin seeds
a pinch of sea salt
Chilli Garlic Chutney (see page 186)
100 g (3½ oz/⅔ cup) roasted unsalted peanuts, crushed
Sesame Raita (see page 205)

VEGETABLES

SPICED SNAKE BEANS WITH PEANUTS

Snake beans (Chinese long beans) are similar to green beans but longer, but if you can't find them, green beans or runner beans would work just as well. The peanuts add a lovely, nutty flavour and I like to serve this with the Chilli Garlic Chutney on page 186.

Blanch the beans in boiling salted water for 2 minutes, then drain.

Heat the butter in a frying pan (skillet) and fry the fennel, cumin, onion, fenugreek and mustard seeds for a minute or so until fragrant. Add the dried chilles, fry for a few more seconds then pour the spices over the beans. Season to taste with salt, and mix all together.

Serve the beans in a large dish, with the roasted peanuts.

SERVES 4

400 g (14 oz) snake beans (Chinese long beans)
a knob of butter
1 teaspoon fennel seeds
1 teaspoon cumin seeds
½ teaspoon onion seeds
½ teaspoon fenugreek seeds
½ teaspoon mustard seeds
200 g (7 oz) dried red chillies
sea salt, to taste
200 g (7 oz/1¼ cups) roasted unsalted peanuts,
    crushed

MALABAR ISTHU WITH PUMPKIN, BITTER GOURD & CAULIFLOWER

This dish orin001ginates from Kerala. It is best compared to a stew and is deliciously creamy and slightly spicy. The bitter gourd (found in nearly every Indian store) adds a lovely bitter-sweet flavour, but if you can't find it, you can use courgette (zucchini) or turnip. You can pair the gourd with almost any vegetable, so a great dish to use whatever veg you have lying around in your fridge!

Heat the oil in a large pan, add the cloves and cinnamon stick and heat gently for 1–2 minutes until fragrant.

Add the onions and cook over a gentle heat for about 10 minutes until translucent. Add the ginger and garlic paste, green chillies and curry leaves and cook for a further 5 minutes. Add the turmeric and cook for a couple of minutes before adding the coconut milk. Bring to the boil then add the cauliflower, gourd and pumpkin. Cover and simmer for about 20 minutes until all the vegetables are tender.

Five minutes before serving, add the tomatoes and pepper, and season to taste with salt and sugar. Garnish with fresh coriander and serve.

SERVES 4

1 tablespoon vegetable oil
1 teaspoon cloves
1 cinnamon stick
2 onions, thinly sliced
1 tablespoon Ginger & Garlic Paste
 (see page 183)
2 green chillies, finely chopped
80 g (3 oz) fresh curry leaves
1 tablespoon ground turmeric
500 ml (17 fl oz/2 cups) coconut milk
150 g (5 oz) cauliflower florets
150 g (5 oz) peeled and diced bitter gourd
150 g (5 oz) peeled and diced pumpkin
100 g (3½ oz) tomatoes, finely chopped
2 teaspoons freshly ground black pepper
sea salt, to taste
sugar to taste
1 bunch of fresh coriander (cilantro), finely
 chopped

MUSTARD GREENS WITH GINGER, GARLIC & CHILLIES

Mustard greens are very similar to spinach in texture. They have a stronger flavour with a distinct mustardy taste, so pair well with Indian spices. This is a great side to any of the meat or fish dishes featured in this book.

Wash the mustard leaves and roughly chop them discarding the stalks.

Heat the oil in a large frying pan (skillet) over a medium heat, and fry the ginger and garlic paste and green chilli paste for a few minutes. Add the mustard greens and cook over a high heat, stirring constantly, for a few minutes until wilted.

Season to taste with salt and serve straight away.

SERVES 4

600 g (1 lb 5 oz) fresh mustard leaves
1 tablespoon vegetable oil
4 teaspoons Ginger & Garlic Paste
  (see page 183)
2 green chillies, blitzed to a paste
sea salt, to taste

155

DESSERTS

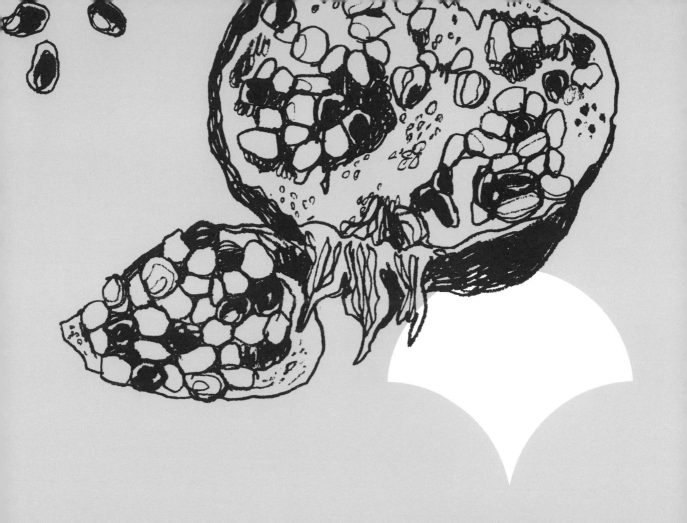

Indian desserts aren't as widely popular
as the main curry dishes, due to the
fact they are mostly very sweet. In India,
however, they are a labour of love, and vary
throughout the country. They are usually
very fragrant and are a perfect way to end
any authentic Indian feast. The desserts we
serve and have featured in this book, all use
classic Indian ingredients but with a few
modern twists; the level of sweetness has
been toned down for the Western palate, so
I hope you enjoy cooking and serving these
as much as the savoury dishes!

JAGGERY TREACLE TART WITH MILK ICE CREAM

Our take on a treacle tart, with the jaggery adding extra richness and sweetness to the dish. You can buy jaggery in most Indian and Western supermarkets but if you don't have any, you can use caster (superfine) sugar, instead.

First, make the ice cream. Put 750 ml (25 fl oz/3 cups) of the milk in a heavy-based saucepan over a medium heat, stirring constantly. Add the sugar and simmer until reduced to 500 ml (17fl oz/2 cups). Turn the heat down to low, add the condensed milk and glucose and stir. Soak the gelatine in cold water until soft. Stir it into the warm milk mixture then add the remaining milk. Leave to cool completely. Transfer to an ice-cream machine and churn for 15–20 minutes, until thickened. Transfer to a freeze-proof container and place in the freezer.

Make the pastry by lightly rubbing the butter into the flour, then mix in the egg. Using your hands, combine to form a smooth dough, adding a tablespoon of water if it's too dry. Shape into a ball, flattern to form a disc, cover with cling film (plastic wrap) and set aside to rest in the refrigerator for 20 minutes.

Preheat the oven to 160°C (320°F/Gas 3) and grease a 23 cm (9 in) flan ring. Roll out the dough on a lightly floured surface to about 5 mm (¼ in) thick and use to line the flan ring. Cover with baking parchment, and bake blind for 20 minutes. Remove the paper and beans and leave to cool in the flan ring. Reduce the oven temperature to 150°C (300°F/Gas 2).

Heat a heavy-based saucepan over a low heat and melt together the syrup, jaggery, lemon juice and eggs. Once everything is incorporated, add the cream. Remove from the heat, then fold in the breadcrumbs. Spoon the mixture into the pastry case and return to the oven for 45 minutes until set and golden. Remove from the oven and allow to cool.

Sprinkle with a little salt and serve with the ice cream.

SERVES 4

200 ml (7 fl oz/scant 1 cup) golden syrup (light corn syrup)
100 g (3½ oz) jaggery, roughly chopped
a squeeze of lemon juice
2 large free-range eggs, beaten
100 ml (3½ fl oz/scant ½ cup) double (heavy) cream
200 g (7 oz/2½ cups) fresh brown breadcrumbs
Himalayan sea salt, to serve

FOR THE ICE CREAM

800 ml (28fl oz) full-fat (whole) milk
75 g (3 oz) caster (superfine) sugar
100 ml (3½ fl oz) condensed milk
1½ teaspoon glucose
1 gelatine sheet

FOR THE PASTRY

110 g (4 oz½ cup) unsalted butter, chilled and diced
225 g (8 oz/1¾ cups) plain (all-purpose) flour, plus extra for dusting
1 large free-range eggs, beaten

NOTE: If you don't have an ice-cream maker, transfer the cooled liquid into a freezer container and put in the freezer for a couple of hours until it starts to solidify. Stir with a spatula to break up the ice crystals, then return it to the freezer. Repeat this process every 30 minutes until the mixture is set.

MISTI DOI WITH POMEGRANATE & MINT

This is a very straightforward recipe that originally hails from Calcutta. Be careful to follow the steps correctly and you can't go wrong. The end result is a creamy, sweet set baked yoghurt with a hint of cardamom.

Preheat the oven to 160°C (320°F/Gas 3).

Place 4 ramekins (custard cups) in a large roasting pan and fill with hot water to come two-thirds up the outer sides of the ramekins.

Combine the condensed milk, yoghurt and ground cardamom in a bowl and mix well.

Divide the mixture among the prepared ramekins and bake in the bain-marie for 6 minutes.

Meanwhile, soak the rose petals in the sugar syrup for a few minutes. Remove and place in a small bowl.

Remove the ramekins from the roasting pan and allow to cool before transferring them to a refrigerator to cool completely.

Garnish with chopped pistachio, pomegranate seeds, sugared-rose petals and mint.

SERVES 4

250 ml (8½ fl oz/1 cup) condensed milk
250 g (9 oz/1 cup) Greek yoghurt
2 teaspoons ground cardamom
50 g (2 oz) rose petals
100 ml (3½ oz/scant ½ cup) sugar syrup
  (see page 220)
4 teaspoons of roughly chopped pistachio nuts
seeds of 1 small pomegranate
a few sprigs of fresh mint leaves, to serve

SHAHI TUKDA WITH BUTTERMILK ICE CREAM

I first came across this dish in Lucknow, where the chef from the Taj Hotel explained to me how when bread became stale, it was then used for this dish by soaking it in sugar syrup to soften it again before deep-frying. It's a good example of resourcefulness that you see so much in India.

First make the buttermilk ice cream. Whisk together the egg yolks and sugar in a large bowl until thick. Heat the cream with half of the lemon zest in a pan until it reaches 85°C (185°F), or until just coming to the boil. Pour over the egg mixture, whisking furiously. Return to the pan over a gentle heat, stirring continuously, until it reaches 82°C (180°F); you should be able to hold your finger in the milk for a couple of seconds. Pour into a bowl placed above iced water and stir until cool. Once cool, fold through the buttermilk. Churn in an ice cream machine according to the manufacturer's instructions until smooth.

To make the custard, whisk together the egg yolks and sugar until thick. Heat the cream with the milk, the vanilla pod and seeds and ground cardamom in a pan until it reaches 85°C (185°F), just before it comes to the boil. Pour into the egg mixture and whisk vigorously. Return to a gentle heat and stir continuously until thickened.

To make the dulce de leche, put the unopened can of condensed milk in a pan, cover with water and boil for 3 hours, topping up with boiling water as necessary. Leave to cool before opening the can and turning out the contents into a bowl.

Soak the brioche in the custard for at least 20 minutes.

Heat the ghee in a frying pan (skillet) and shallow-fry the brioche, in batches, for a few minutes until lightly browned on both sides. Remove from the pan and place on a plate. Top with a scoop of ice cream, drizzle with the dulce de leche, garnish with the pistachios and serve with the berries.

SERVES 10

1 brioche loaf, cut into 10 slices
50 g (2 oz) ghee, for frying
a handful of seasonal berries, to serve
4 tablespoons toasted and crushed pistachio nuts

FOR THE BUTTERMILK ICE CREAM

8 large free-range egg yolks
200 g (7 oz/scant 1 cup) caster (superfine) sugar
600 ml (20 fl oz/scant 2½ cups) double (heavy) cream
zest of 1 lemon
700 ml (24 fl oz/generous 2¾ cups) buttermilk

FOR THE CUSTARD

8 large free-range egg yolks
200 g (7 oz/scant 1 cup) caster (superfine) sugar
600 ml (20 fl oz/scant 2½ cups) double (heavy) cream
300 ml (10 fl oz/scant 1¼ cups) full-fat (whole) milk
1 vanilla pod, split with seeds scraped out
4 pinches of ground cardamom

FOR THE DULCE DE LECHE

400 g (14 oz) can of condensed milk, unopened

NOTE: If you don't have an ice-cream machine, transfer the cooled liquid into a freezer container and put in the freezer for a couple of hours until it starts to solidify. Stir with a spatula to break up the ice crystals, then return it to the freezer. Repeat this process every 30 minutes until the mixture is set.

CARDAMOM KHEER WITH RHUBARB PURÉE & CAROM SEED CRUMBLE

Kheer is basically the Indian equivalent to rice pudding, and is the ultimate comfort food. You can use different varieties of rice if you like, so don't worry if basmati isn't to hand. Make this dish when rhubarb is at its best, for the most wonderful treat.

Soak the rice in cold water for 30 minutes, then strain.

In a heavy-based saucepan, combine the rice, milk and cardamom and cook over a gentle heat for about 15–20 minutes until the rice has absorbed all the milk. Add the cream, jaggery and a little sugar to taste. It should be fairly sweet by this point.

Preheat the oven to 180°C (350°F/Gas 4).

In a separate pan, gently poach the rhubarb in the sugar syrup for about 10 minutes until soft. Strain and blitz in a food processor to form a purée.

To make the carom seed crumble, rub the butter into the flour and sugar in a bowl and mix until you have a breadcrumb-like consistency. Add the carom seeds, then spread the mixture evenly onto a baking sheet and bake for about 20 minutes until lightly toasted.

When ready to serve, spoon the hot rice kheer, with rhubarb purée into bowls and garnished with carom seed crumble.

SERVES 6

400 g (14 oz/2 cups) basmati rice, washed and drained
1 litre (34 fl oz/4 cups) full-fat (whole) milk
5 teaspoons ground cardamom
500 ml (17 fl oz/2 cups) double (heavy) cream
300 g (10½ oz) jaggery, grated
caster (superfine) sugar, to taste
300 g (10½ oz) rhubarb, chopped
300 ml (10 fl oz/scant 1¼ cups) sugar syrup (see page 220)

FOR THE CAROM SEED CRUMBLE

100 g (3½ oz/⅓ cup) unsalted butter, cubed
200 g (7 oz/scant 2 cups) plain (all-purpose) flour
4 tablespoons caster (superfine) sugar
2 teaspoons carom seeds

DESSERTS

ALPHONSO MANGO SORBET WITH CHILLI & COCONUT

Mango is the king of fruit in India, and everyone will tell you Alphonsos are the best of the best. When mango season arrives in India, people go mad for the Alphonso and buy up as much of it as they can get their hands on.

In a saucepan, heat 160 ml (5½ fl oz/¾ cup) water until it reaches boiling point. Remove from the heat, add the lime juice and stir in the sugar until it dissolves. Let the syrup cool for 30 minutes.

Put the mango and 250 ml (8½ fl oz/1 cup) water into a food processor and blitz to form a smooth purée. Add the cooled sugar syrup and blitz briefly again until thoroughly mixed.

Pour the mix into an ice-cream machine and churn to the manufacturer's instructions. If you don't have one, transfer the cooled liquid onto a freeze-proof container and put in the freezer for a couple of hours until it starts to solidify. Stir with a spatula to break up the ice crystals, then return it to the freezer. Repeal this process every 30 minutes until the mixture is set.

The sorbet is best served immediately, sprinkled with the coconut and chilli, but it will freeze for up to 4 days and still taste good.

SERVES 4–5

juice of 2 limes
160 g (5½ oz/¾ cup) caster (superfine) sugar
450 g (1 lb) ripe Alphonso mangoes, destoned and peeled
4 teaspoons toasted coconut flakes
1 red chilli, finely diced, to garnish

ELDERFLOWER & RHUBARB KULFI WITH SESAME BRITTLE

Kulfi is a hard-set ice cream typically made from buffalo milk, which can be seen served roadside throughout India, in various flavours. The best one I've tried is towards the end of Marine Drive in Mumbai. It's the perfect way to cool yourself down on a hot day. The sesame brittle adds a texture and crunch to this dessert — you can buy it ready-made.

Preheat the oven to 180°C (350°F/Gas 4).

Place the rhubarb in an earthenware dish, add 1 tablespoon of the elderflower cordial and roast in the oven for about 20 minutes until soft. Mash the rhubarb and put to one side.

Pour the evaporated milk, condensed milk and cream into a pan and whisk together until well combined. Add the lemon zest. Bring to a bare simmer over a low heat and stir for 5 minutes. Remove from the heat and add the remaining elderflower cordial, mix and leave to cool.

Pour the mixture into a bowl, add the mashed rhubarb and whisk into the infused cream until very well combined and smooth in consistency. Spoon into 4 dariole moulds or ramekin dishes (custard cups). Freeze for at least 4 hours or overnight.

Meanwhile, to make the sesame brittle, line a baking tray with with baking parchment. Heat the sugar in a heavy-based saucepan gently over a medium-low heat, without stirrng, for about 5 minutes until bubbling and golden. Stir in the toasted sesame seeds, boil for a few seconds, then pour onto the prepared baking tray, spreading as thinly as possible. Leave to cool and harden completely. Bash the brittle into small shards.

To loosen the kulfi from the moulds, dip the bottoms of them briefly into hot water, run a knife carefully round the edge of the mould and turn out onto a plate. Top with the shards of sesame brittle and serve.

SERVES 4

200 g (7 oz) rhubarb, chopped into
  1 cm (½ in) pieces
120 ml (4 fl oz/½ cup) elderflower cordial
250 ml (8½ fl oz/1 cup) evaporated milk
250 ml (8½ fl oz/1 cup) condensed milk
250 ml (8½ fl oz/1 cup) double (heavy) cream
1 teaspoon lemon juice

FOR THE SESAME BRITTLE

200 g (7 oz/scant 1 cup) caster (superfine) sugar
4 tablespoons sesame seeds, lightly toasted

SIDES & CHUTNEYS

There are a huge number of chutneys and
pickles throughout India, and the ones we
feature in this chapter can be found all
over the country. They make the most of
vegetables and fruit whether they are in
early stages of growing or if they are in their
peak condition. Either way, making chutneys
and pickles is a fantastic way of preserving
wholesome produce. Rice is also a staple
ingredient in India, served with most dishes.
I have included some simple recipes that
can accompany any of the mains featured
in this book.

TOMATO PILAU

This is a very fragrant rice dish, thanks to the addition of lemongrass and lime leaves. Once cooked, it should be a lovely golden colour. Keep the whole spices in the finished dish, which only adds to the overall presentation.

Wash the rice in cold water, until it runs clear, then leave to soak in warm water for up to 30 minutes until the rice has plumped up. Set aside until needed.

Heat the oil in a large pan. Add the coriander and cumin seeds, along with the cardamom, cinnamon, star anise and fennel seeds and heat for 30 seconds or so until the spices splutter. Add the lemongrass and lime leaves, fry for a few seconds then stir in the the onion and tomato masala and tomato purée.

Mix everything together and cook for 2 minutes before pouring in 1 litre (34 fl oz/4 cups) of water. Season with salt, bring to the boil, then add the drained rice. Cover and cook for about 8 minutes until the rice is tender and all the water has been absorbed. Taste and adjust the seasoning if necessary.

Once cooked, remove from the heat and separate the rice with a fork to avoid clumps. Serve while still warm.

SERVES 8

500 g (1 lb 2 oz/2½ cups) basmati rice
1 tablespoon vegetable oil
1 teaspoon coriander seeds, crushed
1 teaspoon cumin seeds
1 teaspoon green cardamom pods
1 cinnamon stick
2 star anise
1 teaspoon fennel seeds
2 lemongrass stalks
4 Kaffir lime leaves
2 tablespoons Onion & Tomato Masala
  (see page 99)
1 teaspoon tomato purée (paste)
1½ teaspoons sea salt

PILAU RICE

There are many ways to cook rice and everyone believes their own is the best. This is our tried-and-tested method of cooking a perfect rice with a subtle flavour.

SERVES 4

200 g (7 oz/1 cup) basmati rice
1 tablespoon ghee
1 tablespoon cumin seeds
2 fresh Indian bay leaves

Wash the rice in cold water, until it runs clear, then leave to soak in warm water for up to 30 minutes until the rice has plumped up. Drain and set aside.

Heat the ghee in a heavy-based saucepan, add the cumin seeds and bay leaves, and fry for 30 seconds or so until the spices splutter.

Add the drained rice, then cover with 800 ml (28 fl oz/3½ cups) of water and bring to the boil. Cover, reduce the heat and simmer for 20 minutes until tender and all the water has been absorbed.

Serve while still warm.

GUCCI PILAU

This is our designer version of a simple rice, suitable to serve with pretty much any main dish and delicious enough to warrant a designer label.

SERVES 4

200 g (7 oz/1 cup) basmati rice
200 g (7 oz/scant 1 cup) unsalted butter or ghee
1 tablespoon cumin seeds
2 fresh Indian bay leaves
200 g (7 oz) fresh morel mushrooms
a pinch of saffron strands, soaked in a little warm water

Wash the rice in cold water, until it runs clear, then leave to soak in warm water for up to 30 minutes until the rice has plumped up. Drain and set aside.

Heat the ghee in a heavy-based saucepan, add the cumin seeds and bay leaves, then the morels, and fry for 30 seconds or so until the spices splutter.

Add the drained rice and stir, then cover with 800 ml (28 fl oz/3½ cups) of water and add the saffron. Bring to the boil, then cover, reduce the heat and simmer for 20 minutes until the rice is tender and all the water has been absorbed.

Serve while still warm.

GINGER & GARLIC PASTE

I use this in all kinds of recipes as a basic flavouring and it's so much better if you make your own, although ready-made pastes are handy if you are in a hurry.

MAKES 1 KG (2 LB 3 OZ)

500 g (1 lb 2 oz) fresh ginger root, peeled and roughly chopped
500 g (1 lb 2 oz) garlic cloves, peeled
100–200 ml (3½–7 fl oz) vegetable oil

Blitz the ginger and garlic in a blender, gradually adding enough oil to make a smooth paste.

Store in a sterilised jar in the refridgerator. This will keep for up to 2 weeks. You can also store the paste in a freeze-proof container, in the freezer.

PICKLING LIQUOR

I use this to use with all kinds of vegetables but cucumber is a special favourite. It will keep in the refrigerator for several weeks – it keeps forever! If you want to make a smaller amount, the recipe is based on equal quantities of vinegar and sugar.

MAKES 1 LITRE (34 FL OZ/4 CUPS)

500 ml (17 fl oz/2 cups) white wine vinegar
500 g (1 lb 2 oz/2 cups) caster (superfine) sugar
2 star anise
1 cinnamon stick
4 cloves
2 fresh Indian bay leaves

Put all the ingredients in a heavy-based saucepan over a low heat and stir occasionally until all the sugar dissolves.

Remove from the heat and set aside to cool before decanting into a sterilised jar. Store in the fridge until required.

TAMARIND & DATE CHUTNEY

This recipe makes a sweet and sour chutney that matches perfectly with Indian dishes, especially the street food. I use it in my version on Bhel Puri which you can find on page 127, and it makes a great accompaniment to the Jersey Royal Aloo Chaat on page 128.

Boil all the ingredients in a large heavy-based saucepan over a low heat for about 1 hour until well blended and thick. Set aside to cool. If you have used fresh dates, you may need to blitz the chutney in a blender until smooth.

Once cool, store in sterilised jars in the refrigerator for up to 2 weeks. This chutney will also freeze well if you wanted to keep it for longer.

MAKES APPROX. 900 G (1 LB 12 OZ)

500 g (1 lb 2 oz) tamarind paste
2 cinnamon sticks
1 teaspoon black peppercorns
2 fresh Indian bay leaves
300 ml (10 fl oz/scant 1¼ cups) water
2 tablespoons Kashmiri red chilli powder
4 tablespoons date purée or a handful of fresh dates (6–7 dates)
200 g (7 oz) jaggery or caster (superfine) sugar

SIDES & CHUTNEYS

CHILLI GARLIC CHUTNEY

This red-coloured chutney combines dried Kashmiri red chillies with vinegar and garlic to produce a raw, powerful condiment that will liven up any dish.

Soak the dried red chillies in the vinegar overnight, then blitz to a smooth paste.

Blitz the garlic in a blender, gradually adding enough oil to make a smooth paste.

Stir the chilli and garlic paste together and season to taste with sugar and salt.

Store in sterilised jars and keep in the refrigerator until required. It will last for up to 2 weeks. Bring up to room temperature before serving.

MAKES ABOUT 700 G
(1 LB 8 OZ)

500 g (1 lb 2 oz) dried Kashmiri red chillies
500 ml (17 fl oz/2 cups) malt vinegar
200 g (7 oz) garlic cloves, peeled
50 ml (1½ fl oz) vegetable oil
caster (superfine) sugar, to taste
sea salt, to taste

CHILLI GARLIC MAYONNAISE

Soak the chillies in the vinegar overnight before you make the mayo so they soften enough to make a smooth purée.

Put the egg yolks in a high-speed blender. With the motor running, gradually pour in the oil. As the mayonnaise thickens, it can be thinned down with a little water if you like.

Blend in the chilli garlic chutney, then season to taste with sugar, salt and vinegar. The mayonnaise should be glossy and just hold its shape.

Store in sterilised jars and keep in the refrigerator until required. It will last for up to 2 weeks.

MAKES ABOUT 1 LITRE (34 FL OZ/4 CUPS)

4 large free-range egg yolks
1 litre (34 fl oz/4 cups) vegetable oil
2–3 teaspoons Chilli Garlic Chutney (see recipe opposite), depending on how spicy you want it
caster (superfine) sugar, to taste
sea salt, to taste
1 tablespoon malt vinegar

FROM LEFT TO RIGHT:
CHILLI GARLIC MAYONNAISE
(SEE PAGE 189) AND CHILLI GARLIC
CHUTNEY (SEE PAGE 188)

SIDES & CHUTNEYS

COCONUT
& CORIANDER
CHUTNEY

This chutney goes very well with any of the fish dishes featured in this book. It should have a good balance between the coconut and the coriander (cilantro), with the dal (lentils) adding a nutty texture and flavour. This will keep for 1–2 weeks in the refrigerator.

Blitz together the coconut, coriander, ginger and green chillies in a blender with the vegetable oil to bring it together. The consistency should be semi smooth, but you should be able to see specks of white and green, so don't blend it for too long otherwise it'll be too smooth and you will lose the flecked texture.

Separately heat up 4 tablespoons of the vegetable oil in a saucepan over a medium heat. Add the mustard seeds, which will crackle on contact. Next add the curry leaves, dal and dried chillies. Remove from the heat and allow to cool.

Empty the coconut and coriander chutney into a mixing bowl, fold in the cooled spices and lime juice, then season to taste with salt and a little sugar.

MAKES ABOUT 500 G
(1 LB 2OZ)

200 g (7 oz) fresh grated coconut
200 g (7 oz) fresh coriander (cilantro)
a thumb-size piece of fresh ginger root, peeled
2 green chillies
100 ml (3½ fl oz) vegetable oil, plus
    4 tablespoons
1 teaspoon black or yellow mustard seeds
a handful of fresh curry leaves
2 teaspoons channa dal (yellow chickpea lentils)
4 dried Kashmiri red chillies
6 tablespoons lime juice
sea salt, to taste
caster (superfine) sugar, to taste

GOOSEBERRY CHUTNEY

This chutney pairs beautifully with mackerel (see page 44) and can be used with other fish dishes, or even some game dishes.

Heat the oil in a heavy-based pan, add the fennel and onion seeds and the chillies and stir, then add the ground turmeric and cook for a further 30 seconds, stirring constantly to prevent it from burning.

Add the gooseberries, reduce the heat and cook for 20 minutes until you achieve a jammy consistency.

Season to taste with a little salt and plenty of sugar to balance out the sourness of the gooseberries.

Store in sterilised jars and keep in the refrigerator until required. It will last for up to 2 weeks.

MAKES ABOUT 450 G (1 LB)

200 ml (7 fl oz/scant 1 cup) vegetable oil
1 teaspoon fennel seeds
1 teaspoon onion seeds
3 dried Kashmiri red chillies
2 teaspoons ground turmeric
500 g (1 lb 2 oz) fresh or frozen gooseberries
sea salt, to taste
caster (superfine) sugar, to taste

CORIANDER & MINT CHUTNEY

This is a classic chutney and goes so well with so many Indian dishes. It can also work well as a marinade to lamb.

MAKES ABOUT 1.5 KG (3 LB 5 OZ)

1 kg (2 lb 3 oz) fresh coriander (cilantro), stems and leaves
500 g (1 lb 2 oz) fresh mint leaves
4 green chillies
a thumb-size piece of fresh ginger root
2 garlic cloves, peeled
5 tablespoons lemon juice
200 ml (7 fl oz/scant 1 cup) vegetable oil
caster (superfine) sugar, to taste
sea salt, to taste

Put the coriander, mint, green chillies, ginger, garlic and lemon juice in a blender, then, with the motor running, gradually pour in the oil and blitz until the mixture is a smooth consistency.

Season to taste with sugar and salt. Store in sterilised jars in the refrigerator for up to 1 week. This chutney will also freeze well.

CORIANDER CHUTNEY

If you are making larger batch of this chutney, omit the lemon juice, sugar and salt until just before serving. This will allow the chutney to retain its colour.

MAKES ABOUT 450 G (1 LB)

500 g (1 lb 2 oz) fresh coriander (cilantro), stems and leaves
200 ml (7 fl oz/scant 1 cup) vegetable oil
a thumb-size piece of fresh ginger root
4 garlic cloves, peeled
2 green chillies
6 tablespoons lemon juice
caster (superfine) sugar, to taste
sea salt, to taste

Blitz the coriander in a food procressor with the oil, ginger, garlic and green chillies until it forms a fine paste.

Add the lemon juice and season to taste with sugar and salt. Store in sterilised jars in the refrigerator for up to 1 week. This chutney will also freeze well.

PEANUT
CHUTNEY

We serve this chutney with the Duck Leg Kathi Roll on page 111 but it goes especially well with chicken, too. It should last for up to two weeks in the refrigerator, but bring it to room temperature to serve. It will also keep for longer in the freezer.

Blitz the peanuts and sesame seeds to a semi-fine powder in a food processor, then gradually add enough of the vegetable oil to make a thick chutney consistency that will just be able to hold its shape at room temperature.

Add the lemon juice and chilli powder, then season to taste with sugar and salt. Store in a sterilised jar in the refrigerator until needed.

MAKES ABOUT 500 G (1 LB 2OZ)

500 g (1 lb 2 oz/generous 3 cups) roasted
    unsalted peanuts
200 g (7 oz/1¼ cups) white sesame seeds,
    roasted
200 ml (7 fl oz/scant 1 cup) vegetable oil
100 ml (3½ fl oz/scant ½ cup) lemon juice
2 teaspoons Kashmiri red chilli powder
caster (superfine) sugar, to taste
sea salt, to taste

SIDES & CHUTNEYS

PINEAPPLE PICKLE

Sweet, sour and spicy, this chutney can be paired with game dishes, tandoori fish or paneer.

MAKES ABOUT 450 G (1 LB)

200 ml (7 fl oz/scant 1 cup) vegetable oil
1 tablespoon mustard seeds
a handful of fresh curry leaves
4 dried Kashmiri red chillies
2 teaspoons Kashmiri red chilli powder
1 teaspoon ground turmeric
500 g (1 lb 2 oz) pineapple flesh, diced
100 ml (3½ fl oz/scant ½ cup) white wine vinegar
caster (superfine) sugar, to taste
sea salt, to taste
1 teaspoon ground mustard seeds
1 teaspoon ground fenugreek

Heat the oil in a large heavy-based frying pan (skillet) over a mendium heat. Add the mustard seeds and fry for 30 seconds or so until they start to splutter, then add the curry leaves, chillies, chilli powder and turmeric and cook for a minute or so, taking care that the spices do not burn.

Add the pineapple and vinegar, and season to taste with sugar and salt. Reduce the heat to low and cook for about 20 minutes until half the pineapple has become a rough purée while the rest retains its shape. Add the ground mustard seed and fenugreek to the pan and stir well. Leave to cool, then spoon into clean jars, cover and refrigerate.

Store in sterilised jars in the refrigerator for up to 2–3 weeks.

GINGER PICKLE

Typically served as part of larger thali, only a small amount needs to be used as it has a very powerful flavour.

MAKES ABOUT 500 G (1 LB 2 OZ)

1 kg (2 lb 3 oz) fresh ginger root, sliced with skin on
200 ml (7 fl oz/scant 1 cup) vegetable oil
1 tablespoon black mustard seeds
a handful of fresh curry leaves
3 dried Kashmiri red chillies
2 teaspoons Kashmiri red chilli powder
3 teaspoons tamarind paste
5 teaspoons grated jaggery or caster (superfine) sugar
sea salt, to taste

Pour the oil in a heavy-based saucepan, and heat until it is about 180°C (350°F). The oil is hot enough when a cube of bread sizzles when dropped into it.

Deep-fry the ginger in the hot oil for a few minutes until all the moisture has left the ginger and it turns a light brown colour. Lift the ginger out of the oil with a slotted spoon and leave to cool slightly on kitchen paper, then blend in a food processor into a smooth paste.

Temper the oil by re-heating it gently with the mustard seeds, curry leaves, dried chillies and chilli powder, then fold the oil into the ginger paste. Mix in the tamarind and jaggery and season to taste with salt.

Store in sterilised jars in the refrigerator for up to 2–3 weeks.

CURRY LEAF MAYONNAISE

Depending on how much mayonnaise you want to make, you can change the volume of the oil and its tempering, as it stores well in the refrigerator for a week or so. You make the flavoured oil first, then use it to make the mayonnaise. The ratio is about 2 eggs yolks to 500 ml (17 fl oz/2 cups) of oil. Adding a little lemon juice near the start can help to prevent the mayonnaise from splitting.

To make the curry leaf oil, pour the oil in a heavy-based saucepan or *kadai*, and heat until it is about 180°C (350°F). The oil is hot enough when a cube of bread sizzles when dropped into it. Add the mustard seeds, curry leaves, chillies and ground turmeric, then remove from the heat and leave to cool and infuse.

To make the mayonnaise, put the egg yolks and lemon juice in a blender. With the motor running, gradually pour in the curry leaf oil and blitz together until the mixture thickens and emulsifies. Add the mustard seeds, curry leaves, chillies and turmeric, then season to taste with sugar, salt and a little more lemon juice if you like. The mayonnaise should be shiny and just hold its shape.

Store in a sterilised jar in the refrigerator for up to a week.

MAKES 1 LITRE (35 FL OZ)

FOR THE CURRY LEAF OIL
(MAKES 2.5 LITRES (88 FL OZ/10 CUPS)

2.5 litres (88 fl oz/10 cups) vegetable oil
1 tablespoon mustard seeds
160 g (5½ oz) of fresh curry leaves
2½ dried Kashmiri red chillies
2½ teaspoons ground turmeric

FOR THE CURRY LEAF MAYONNAISE

4 large free-range egg yolks
a splash of lemon juice
1 litre (34 fl oz/4 cups) curry leaf oil (see above)
2 tablespoons black mustard seeds
a handful of fresh curry leaves
5 dried Kashmiri red chillies
2 teaspoons ground turmeric
caster (superfine) sugar, to taste
sea salt, to taste

WILD GARLIC CHUTNEY

Every spring my mother gathers huge quantities of wild garlic from the woods around our Sussex home, in the UK. Kilos of the young leaves are brought to the restaurant and blitzed into oil and frozen, which we have found is the best way to keep wild garlic. It affects neither the colour nor the taste, and from there it can easily be made into a chutney. Towards the middle of the season, the flowers of the plant are perfect for garnishes, with their hot, intense flavour, or they can be left to ferment for use later in the year.

Put the coriander, wild garlic, green chillies, ginger and garlic in a blender, then, with the motor running, gradually pour in the oil until you reach a smooth consistency. Add the lemon juice and season to taste with sugar and salt. Store in the refrigerator for up to a week.

If you need to keep it for longer, omit the lemon juice and add just before serving.

MAKES ABOUT 1 KG (2 LB 3 OZ)

500 g (1 lb 2 oz) fresh coriander (cilantro), stems and leaves
500 g (1 lb 2 oz) wild garlic leaves
4 green chillies
a thumb-size piece of fresh ginger root
2 garlic cloves, peeled
200 ml (7 fl oz/scant 1 cup) vegetable oil
5 tablespoons lemon juice
caster (superfine) sugar, to taste
sea salt, to tase

SHALLOT & GINGER RAITA

To achieve the right consistency, it is important that you hang the yoghurt before making this raita. This is a perfect accompaniment with almost any dish.

First, hang the yoghurt by turning it out of its packaging straight into a muslin (cheesecloth), tie the ends and hang it over a dish for 1 hour. Make sure the yoghurt isn't stirred or disturbed otherwise you will lose it through the muslin.

Mix all the remaining ingredients into the yoghurt, seasoning to taste with more sugar than salt to balance the acidity of the yoghurt. Keep in the refrigerator until needed.

Store in an airtight container and keep refrigerated for up to a week. Bring to room temperature before serving.

MAKES ABOUT 600 G (1 LB 5 OZ)

500 g (1 lb 2 oz/2 cups) Greek yoghurt
2 banana shallots, finely chopped
a thumb-size piece of fresh ginger root, finely chopped
2 tablespoons fresh mint, cut into julienne strips
2 tablespoons finely chopped fresh coriander (cilantro)
1 tablespoon cumin seeds, toasted
caster (superfine) sugar, to taste
sea salt, to taste

SESAME RAITA

We serve this in the restaurant alongside a purée of smoked aubergine (eggplant). Tahini isn't strictly Indian but sesame seeds are used frequently in Indian cooking. You can make your own tahini by blending roasted sesame seeds with vegetable oil.

To hang the yoghurt, turn it out of its packaging straight into a muslin (cheesecloth), tie the ends and hang it over a dish for 1 hour. Make sure the yoghurt isn't stirred or disturbed otherwise you will lose it through the muslin.

Mix the tahini and garlic paste into the yoghurt, and season to taste with sugar and salt.

Store in an airtight container and keep refrigerated for up to a week. Bring to room temperature before serving.

MAKES ABOUT 600 G (1 LB 5 OZ)

500 g (1 lb 2 oz/2 cups) Greek yoghurt
200 g (7 oz/¾ cup) tahini paste
50 g (2 oz) store-bought garlic paste
caster (superfine) sugar, to taste
sea salt, to taste

PUMPKIN CHUTNEY

This is a lovely chutney, slightly sweet from the pumpkin, that is best served in autumn alongside any game dish.

MAKES ABOUT 350 G (12 OZ)

100 ml (3½ fl oz/scant ½ cup) vegetable oil,
    plus 1 tablespoon, for frying
½ teaspoon ground turmeric
1 teaspoon Kashmiri red chilli powder
1 teaspoon ground cumin
300 g (10½ oz) peeled, seeded and diced pumpkin
1 teaspoon black mustard seeds
10 fresh curry leaves
1 teaspoon cumin seeds
2 dried Kashmiri red chillies
sea salt, to taste

Preheat the oven to 160°C (320°F/Gas 3).

In a roasting pan, mix the oil with the turmeric, chilli powder and ground cumin, then toss in the pumpkin and coat. Roast in the oven for around 20 minutes until soft. Allow to cool, then blitz in a food processor to a purée.

Heat a little oil in a saucepan, add the mustard seeds and when they start to splutter, add the curry leaves, cumin seeds and chillies and remove from the heat.

Strain the oil into the pumpkin and season to taste with salt.

Store in an airtight container and keep refrigerated for up 2 weeks. Bring to room temperature before serving.

208

PUMPKIN PICKLE

In contrast to the pumpkin chutney, this pickle is great for using up surplus vegetables. It is best served alongside fish and game, or simply with bread and yoghurt as a light lunch.

MAKES ABOUT 400 G (14 OZ)

100 ml (3½ fl oz/scant ½ cup) vegetable oil
2 teaspoons onion seeds
4 dried Kashmiri red chillies
1 Delica pumpkin, peeled, seeded and finely diced
1 tablespoon Kashmiri red chilli powder
1 teaspoon ground turmeric
200 ml (7 fl oz/scant 1 cup) white distilled vinegar
100 g (3½ oz) jaggery or caster (superfine) sugar

In a deep heavy-based saucepan, heat the oil over a medium heat, add the onion seeds and dried chillies and stir to infuse with the spices.

Add the pumpkin and cook over a low heat for about 10–15 minutes until the pumpkin is almost cooked. Then add the chilli powder and turmeric and cook for a further 2 minutes. Finally, add the vinegar and jaggery and cook for about 5 minutes until all the liquid from the vinegar has evaporated. Remove from the heat, allow to cool, and store in a sterilised jar for up 2–3 weeks.

SIDES & CHUTNEYS

PANEER

In the restaurant we like to make soft crumbly paneer, as opposed to the solid blocks you see in most supermarkets. If you would like a firmer texture, press the cheese with a weight in the refrigerator for a few hours.

In a deep, large, heavy-based saucepan, gently bring the milk to the boil, stirring constantly to prevent the milk from sticking and burning on the bottom of the pan.

Once the milk has come to the boil, add the lemon juice. You should see the mixture separate into white solids and an almost green liquid. Remove from the heat.

At this stage, season to taste with a little salt, then strain through a muslin (cheesecloth) cloth. Leave to drain for 1 hour until all the liquid has been removed, and what you should be left with is a soft, fresh, crumbly paneer.

Cover and store in the refrigerator until needed. It will keep for up to a week.

MAKES ABOUT 400 G (14 OZ)

6 litres (210 fl oz/24 cups) full-fat (whole) milk
5 tablespoons lemon juice
sea salt, to taste

GUNPOWDER

You can use this as a dry spice mix (see photo, top left) or blend it with the toasted sesame oil to create a wet spice mix (see photo, central). At the restaurant, we serve this on top of roasted sweet potato but it can be used as an accompaniment to any south Indian dish.

Preheat the oven to 150°C (300°F/Gas 2).

For a dry spice mix, lay all the ingredients except the oil on a baking tray and roast in the oven for 20 minutes. Allow the spices to cool before blitzing in a food processor, into a fine powder. For a wet spice mix, as pictured, blend the powder with the sesame oil.

Store in a sterilised jar the refrigerator until needed. It will keep for 1–2 weeks.

MAKES ABOUT 350 G (12 OZ)

250 g (9 oz/1 cup) channa dal
  (yellow chickpea lentils)
a handful of whole dried Kashmiri red chillies
1 tablespoon coriander seeds
1 tablespoon cumin seeds
1 tablespoon black sesame seeds
a handful of fresh curry leaves
100 g (3½ oz/⅔ cup) salted peanuts
300 ml (10 fl oz/scant 1¼ cups) toasted
  sesame oil (optional)

TOMATO CHUTNEY

If you want to make your own tamarind paste, soak a 5 cm (2 in) slice of fresh tamarind in three tablespoons of warm water for three minutes. Squeeze the tamarind, then drain the juice and discard the fibre.

Heat the oil in a large heavy-based frying pan (skillet), add the onions and fry for about 10 minutes until soft. Add the tomatoes, garlic, cumin seeds, chilli powder and salt and continue to cook for a further 10–15 minutes until the tomatoes soften and break down. Remove the pan from the heat and leave to cool.

Grind the mixture in a pestle and motar, with 4 tablespoons of water to a smooth paste, and keep aside.

For the seasoning, heat the oil, add the mustard seeds and fry for 30 seconds or so until they start to splutter. Add the chillies and curry leaves and fry for a few more minutes until the spices have infused in the oil.

Pour the ground tomato paste into the seasoning and mix in the tamarind paste. Add 2 tablespoons more water to thin down the chutney and stir well to combine. Bring to the boil, season to taste with a little more salt, allow to cool a little and serve.

Store in a sterilised jar the refrigerator until needed. It will keep for up to a week.

MAKES ABOUT 350 G (12 OZ)

1 tablespoon vegetable oil
10 small onions, chopped
4 tomatoes, chopped
2 garlic cloves, minced
1 teaspoon cumin seeds
¾ teaspoon Kashmiri red chilli powder
a pinch of sea salt
2 teaspoons tamarind paste

FOR SEASONING

1 tablespoon vegetable oil
1 teaspoon black mustard seeds
2 whole dried Kashmiri red chillies
2–3 fresh curry leaves

BURNT ONION RAITA

The idea is to burn the shallots until they are completely blistered and there is no moisture left (see photo on page 87). This way you will achieve a very fine powder to add to the yoghurt. The result is a delicious, smoky raita that goes well with grilled meat. If you can't find shallots, this recipe works just as well with regular brown onions.

Preheat the oven to 200°C (400°F/Gas 6).

Place the shallots, cut-side down, on a baking tray and cook in the oven for 2–3 hours, or at least until all the moisture has gone. You want to burn the onions to a fine ash so don't be too worried when they come out black from the oven! Leave to cool, then blitz to a fine powder in a food processor. Combine the burnt onion powder with the yoghurt, then season to taste with sugar and salt.

Store in an airtight container and keep refrigerated for up to a week.

SERVES 10

1 kg (2 lb 3 oz) shallots, halved
500 g (1 lb 2 oz/2 cups) Greek yoghurt
caster (superfine) sugar, to taste
sea salt, to taste

SIDES & CHUTNEYS

DRINKS

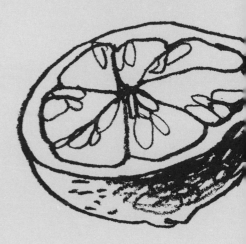

I have to thank my bar manager, Will Rogers, for the benefit of his expertise in this section and we have chosen a few of the most popular cocktails at the bar. I'd also like to thank Sam Paget Steavenson from The Rum Runner, London, who helped us in creating the original cocktails when we first opened in Brixton and Soho.

The cocktails at Kricket are not like a glass of wine that we try to pair with the food. Instead, we simply infuse some of the classic spices and flavours with good-quality booze, to bring you a taste of India with every sip. Subtle hints of clove, curry leaf and turmeric can all be found in these cocktails; the key is to keep it simple. You do not have to be a bartending pro to make these drinks – the key is to lead with your taste buds, and have fun creating them! Most of the drinks serve one, so for accuracy, weigh out your measures in grams (ounces) using electric scales.

Although it's nice to serve a cocktail in the appropriate glassware, it's not the end of the world if you don't have a fancy coupe or a rocks glass, in the cupboard; just grab what you have and improvise. Remember, though, that some drinks should be served neat, so do look at the method for those that require ice in the glass and those that don't.

ANAR DANA

If you like pomegranate and you like tequila, then you will love this. If you cant get hold of fresh pomegranate juice, muddling the fresh seeds will do just fine.

SERVES 1

50 g (2 oz) good-quality tequila
25 g (1 oz) fresh pomegranate juice
  (or pomegranate seeds, muddled)
a squeeze of fresh lime juice
20 g (¾ oz) sugar syrup
½ teaspoon rose water
5 dashes of cardamom bitters

TO SERVE

ice cubes
soda water
1 sprig of mint
a few pomegranate seeds

Add the tequila, pomegranate juice or muddled seeds, lime juice, rose water and cardamom bitters to a cocktail shaker.

Shake and double-strain into a tall glass filled with ice cubes.

Top up with soda water. Garnish with the mint sprig and sprinkle with pomegranate seeds.

SUGAR SYRUP

A lot of my cocktails use a simple sugar syrup which can be made in advance, and kept in the fridge. It will last for about 1 month.

MAKES 750 ML (25 FL OZ)

750 ml (25 fl oz/3 cups) filtered water
750 g (1 lb 10 oz/4 cups) caster (superfine) sugar

To make a simple sugar syrup, just put the water in a large heavy-based saucepan with the sugar.

Heat until the sugar dissolves, then boil for 15 minutes.

Leave to cool, then store in a sterilised glass bottle – a screw-topped wine bottle is excellent. Keep in the refrigerator until required. This syrup lasts for a very long time if stored correctly.

DRINKS

MANGIFERA

If there is one fruit from India that must be showcased it's the mango. The mango pulp works perfectly in this cocktail, providing the rich sweetness you want from this intense fruit. Combine this with the heat from the green chilli and it's a match made in heaven.

SERVES 1

50 g (2 oz) good-quality spiced rum
25 g (1 oz) fresh mango pulp
a squeeze of fresh lime juice
a dash of agave syrup
1 cm (½ in) fresh green chilli

TO SERVE

ice cubes
lime wheel
2 pinches of ground pink peppercorns

Add the spiced rum, mango pulp, lime juice, agave syrup and green chilli to a cocktail shaker.

Shake and double-strain into a rocks glass (tumbler) filled with ice.

Garnish with a lime wheel sprinkled with ground pink peppercorns.

LUCKY NEEM

The curry leaf is the key here; if you can get hold of this you have a very special cocktail. This is a twist on a drink I made a thousand times working in a certain Soho members' club.

SERVES 1

6 fresh curry leaves
3 slices of cucumber
50 g (2 oz) good-quality oriental spiced gin
25 g (1 oz) fresh lime juice
20 g (¾ oz) sugar syrup (see page 222)

Put 5 of the curry leaves and 2 slices of cucumber into a cocktail shaker and gently press with a muddler to release the aromas and flavour.

Add the gin, lime juice and sugar syrup. Shake and double-strain into a coupe.

Garnish by floating the remaining cucumber and curry leaf on top.

SPICED MASALA CHAI

This recipe was given to me by my good friend, Rob Laurie. Found on virtually every street corner in the country. Intensely sweet and frangrantly spiced, you should get a kick from the ginger at the back of your throat as you drink it.

Add the cloves, ginger, cardamom pods, cinnamon and water into a large saucepan. Bring to the boil on a medium-high heat. Let it boil for 2 minutes. Add the tea bags and leave to simmer for 30 minutes or more if you have time. (The longer the better.)

Pour in the condensed milk and stir so it doesn't stick to the bottom of the pan. Bring up the heat to reach boil. Keep stirring so not to burn.

Just as it begins to bubble take it off the heat, strain into cups and serve immediately, while it is still piping hot.

Sweeten with sugar, if required. (But it should be sweet enough!)

SERVES 6–8

2 cloves
200 g (7 oz) fresh ginger, thinly sliced
25 green cardamom pods
2 sticks of cinnamon
1 litre (34 fl oz) water
175 ml (6 oz) condensed milk
5 good-quality tea bags
caster (superfine) sugar, to taste (optional)

DRINKS

PLUMMAHARAJA

Find that old bottle of Calvados that is kicking about and create something special. As for the infusion, it's simple and the end result rich and subtly spiced. I love to infuse a whole bottle of vodka and have it ready to use, whenever I need it. For the best flavour, make sure you use a good-quality brand vodka.

To make the cardamom-infused vodka, drop the cardamom pods into the bottle of vodka. Leave for 24 hours to infuse, then strain out the pods.

To make the cocktail, put the ginger in a shaker and press with a muddler. Add the remaining ingredients and shake.

Strain into a highball glass filled with ice cubes. Garnish with the plum slice and mint sprig.

SERVES 1

FOR THE CARDAMOM-INFUSED VODKA (MAKES 700 ML/23½ FL OZ)

10 green cardamom pods
700 ml (23½ fl oz) bottle of good-quality vodka

FOR THE PLUMMAHARAJA

40 g (1½ oz) fresh ginger root
3 tablespoons cardamom-infused vodka
  (see above)
20 g (¾ oz) Calvados
40 g (1½ oz) fresh red plum juice
a generous squeeze of lemon juice
a dash of agave syrup
2 dashes of orange bitters

TO SERVE

ice cubes
1 slice of fresh plum, to garnish
1 sprig of fresh mint, to garnish

MANGO LASSI

Lassi comes mainly in two varieties: sweet and salted. This fruity, mango version is the sweet kind, and is slightly spiced with cumin, peppercorns and saffron, for added flavour.

To make the lassi, add the mango pulp, water and yoghurt to a large bowl and whisk until it becomes a smooth, thick consistency. You may need to use a handblender to do this. Add the cumin, pink peppercorns and salt, and stir again. Cover and leave in fridge to cool.

Serve in a tall glass with a few ice cubes. Garnish with finely diced mango, mint and a pinch of saffron.

SERVES 10

750 ml (1 lb 2 oz) fresh mango pulp
375 ml (12½ fl oz) water
4 Tablespoons of Greek style yoghurt
4 pinches of ground cumin
7 pinches of ground pink Peppercorn
7 pinches of pink Himalayan sea salt

TO SERVE

ice cubes
half a mango, peeled, destoned and finely diced
a sprig of fresh mint
a pinch of saffron

DRINKS

YELLOW
FAIRY

A cocktail that could be healthy? The fresh turmeric definitely helps and also turns the drink a bright, vibrant yellow that can't be resisted, while the egg white gives it the smooth head similar to a whisky sour.

Pour the Absinthe into your coup, swirl aroud to coat the inside, then dicard.

Put the turmeric in a cocktail shaker and press with a muddler to release the juices. Add the gin, sugar syrup and lemon juice, then add the egg white.

Shake vigorously to create a smooth foam. Add ice and shake again. Double-strain into your prepared coupe.

Float an edible flower on top for an extra flourish, if you like.

SERVES 1

15 g (½ oz) Absinthe
3 small slices of fresh turmeric
3 tablespoons good-quality gin
2 tablespoons sugar syrup (see page 222)
2 tablespoons lemon juice
1 egg white
ice cubes
edible flower, to garnish (optional)

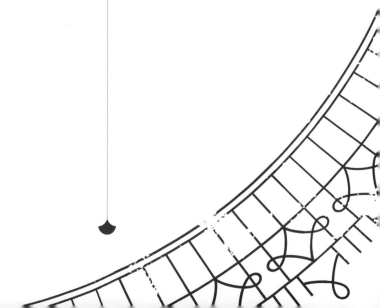

SMOKED TARBOOZ

A vodka-based cocktail always gives stage to all the other flavours. Watermelon and cinnamon work together beautifully. And if you have some single malt whisky kicking about, it really brings a whole other layer to the drink.

To make the cinnamon syrup, bring the water to the boil in a large heavy-based saucepan. Add the sugar and stir until it dissolves, then add the cinnamon sticks and leave to simmer for 15 minutes. Take the saucepan off the heat and leave to cool. Once cooled, strain and decant into a seterilsed glass bottle. An empty wine bottle with a screw-top is perfect.

To make the smoked tarbooz, put all the ingredients into a cocktail shaker. Shake and double-strain into rocks glass filled with ice cubes.

Using a pipette dropper filled with a single malt, drop 6 drops onto the ice for a aromatic, smoky finish on the nose. Garnish with the bay leaf just before serving.

SERVES 1

**FOR THE CINNAMON SYRUP
(MAKES 750 ML/26 FL OZ)**

750ml (25 fl oz) filtered water
750 g (1 lb 10 oz/3 cups) caster
 (superfine) sugar
50 g (2 oz) cinnamon sticks

FOR THE SMOKED TARBOOZ

50 g (2 oz) good-quality vodka
35 g (1 oz) fresh watermelon juice
a squeeze of fresh lime juice
15 g (½ oz) cinnamon syrup (see above)

TO SERVE

ice cubes
6 drops of Lagavulin or other single malt whisky
1 fresh or dried Indian bay leaf

OLD NARANGI

For those of you who like to sip on an Old Fashioned, you will love this. Just choose your favourite bourbon.

To make the cardamom-infused bourbon, drop the cardamom pods into the bottle. (You may have to take a shot before so they fit!) Screw the top back on and leave the bottle on its side for 48 hours. Strain out the pods and fill the bottle back up.

To maked the cocktail, put the marmalade in a shaker. Add the cardamom-infused bourbon, lemon juice and syrup and stir to dissolve the marmalade. Add ice and shake.

Double-strain into a rocks glass filled with ice. Garnish with the orange slice.

SERVES 1

FOR THE CARDAMOM-INFUSED BOURBON (MAKES 700 ML/23½ FL OZ)

40 green cardamom pods
700 ml (23½ fl oz) good-quality bourbon

FOR THE OLD NARANGI

50 g (2 oz) good-quality orange marmalade
3 tablespoons cardamom-infused bourbon (see above)
2 tablespoons fresh lemon juice
2 teaspoons sugar syrup (see page 222)
Ice cubes

TO SERVE

ice cubes
1 slice of orange

HIMALAYAN PINE

If you can get hold of Pino Mugo, a pine liqueur from Italy, you will create a long, refreshing drink with aromas to put you in the foot hills of the Himalayas. Well, kind of... If you can't get Pino Mugo, try it with a premium gin.

Add all the Calvados, peach liqueur, Pine Mugom sugar syrup, lemon juice, salt and kewra water to a cocktial shaker.

Shake and strain into a tall glass filled with ice.

Top up with soda water and garnish with a fresh pine sprig.

SERVES 1

50 g (2 oz) Calvados
10 g (¼ oz) peach liqueur
10 g (¼ oz) Pino Mugo or another premium gin
10 g (¼ oz) sugar syrup (see page 222)
20 g (¾ oz) lemon juice
a pinch of Himalayan salt
½ teaspoon kewra water

TO SERVE
ice cubes
soda water
1 sprig of pine

239

PINKS

A very seasonal drink, but when rhubarb is in, be sure to make full use of it in this refreshing and sophisticated tipple.

SERVES 1

**FOR THE RHUBARB SYRUP
(MAKES 1 LITRE/34 FL OZ/4 CUPS)**

1 litre (34 fl oz/4 cups) filtered water
1 kg (2 lb 3 oz/4 cups) caster (superfine) sugar
5 sticks of rhubarb, halved or quartered
1 star anise
5 green cardamom pods

FOR THE PINK

3 slices of fresh red chilli
50 g (2 oz) good-quality gin
35 g (1 oz) rhubarb syrup (see above)
15 g (½ oz) lemon juice
ice-cold soda water, to serve

To make the rhubarb syrup, bring the water to the boil in a deep, heavy-based saucepan. Add the sugar and stir until it has dissolved. Lower the heat and add the rhubarb, star anise and cardamom pods.

Leave to simmer for 20 minutes or until the rhubarb has cooked through. You should be left with a very pink rhubarb-flavoured sugar syrup with a hint of star anise and cardamom. Leave to cool, then strain and decant into a sterilised glass bottle.

Drop the red chilli slices into a shaker and press with a muddle until they are broken up. Add the gin, rhubarb syrup and lemon juice. Shake and double-strain into chilled champagne flute.

Top up with ice-cold soda water, to serve.

SWEET & SALTY FRESH LIME SODA

The classic Indian soft drink and is extremely refreshing – the only question is do you like it sweet or salted? See recipe photo on next page.

SERVES 1

25 g (1 oz) fresh lime juice
20 g (¾ g) tablespoons sugar syrup (see page 222)
ice cubes

TO SERVE

3 pinches Himalayan pink salt (optional)
soda water
1 sprig of mint (optional)

Put the lime juice and sugar syrup into a tall glass and add ice.

Add the salt, if you fancy. Top up with soda water and give it a quick mix.

For added freshness, you can garnish your soda with a sprig of mint.

ACKNOWLEDGEMENTS

We would like to thank our families and friends who were there in support from the day we first opened in Brixton. They helped us get off the ground and spread the word to a wider audience. We'd also like to thank our fantastic staff, from the kitchen and front of house to the kitchen porters, who work tirelessly every day to make the restaurant what it is today. Without them this wouldn't have been possible.

—WILL BOWLBY & RIK CAMPBELL

A lot of time and effort went into the organisation and production of this book, so a big thank you to everyone who has helped along the way: I'd like to start by thanking my agent, Charile Brotherstone, who believed in this project from the start; Pierre Koffmann for taking the time to write the foreword; my Publishers, Hardie Grant, especially my commissioning editor, Kajal Mistry, for giving me the opportunity to publish this book. A huge thanks needs to go to my photography team Hugh Johnson and Dave Gatenby for the amazing photos and for the support you have shown me and Kricket, from day one, and of course, the incredible design team Run For The Hills, in particular, Chris Trotman and Myoung Chung, for their creative vision and slick design. A massive thank you to my team of food stylists: Laurie Perry and Natalie Thomson, who went above and beyond during the planning and preparation during the shoot – I could not have got through it without you. I would also like to thank Linda Berlin for prop styling, my recipe editor, the ever patient Wendy Hobson, for whipping my copy into shape! And last, but not least, thank you to every single one of you, for showing Kricket support, whether it has been through dining at the restaurants to buying this book – without you, this could not be have been possible. Thank you!

—WILL BOWLBY

ABOUT
KRICKET

Kricket first launched as a tiny 20-seat restaurant set inside a shipping container in Brixton, London. Co-founded by head chef Will Bowlby and front of house Rik Campbell, Kricket combines the best of British seasonal ingredients with the authentic flavours of India, in a relaxed and informal space.

Opening as one of the main food offerings at POP Brixton, the small, neighborhood restaurant proved to be a recipe for success, and after only a year of trading picked up a string of accolades, whilst becoming a firm favourite amongst celebrity chefs, including Pierre Koffmann and Michel Roux Jr. After almost two years the restaurant in a shipping container closed its doors and relocated to a bigger site in the heart of London in Soho in 2017. An evolution of the Brixton-born concept Kricket Soho brings to life refined Indian dishes that aim to be both seasonal and accessible.

Full of authenticity, experience, talent, passion and hard work, Kricket's twist on classic Indian dishes and cocktails has amassed a loyal following. Answering our insatiable appetite for modern Indian food, it will take you right back to Mumbai where the story started.

Within its first year, Kricket Soho was awarded a Bib Gourmand by The Michelin Guide, and won best newcomer in The Asian Curry Awards.

ABOUT
THE
AUTHOR

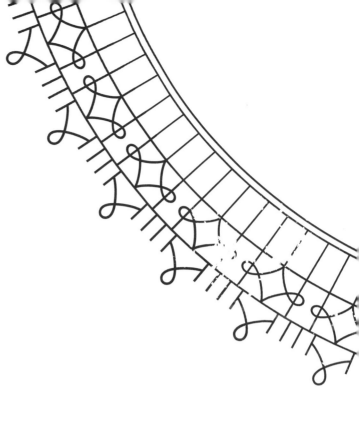

Will Bowlby, head chef and co-founder of Kricket, has brought a new vision to the UK's Indian food scene. Shortlisted for Young British Foodies 'Chef of the year' category for two years in a row, Will started his culinary career at Le Café Anglais, working under the guidance of Rowley Leigh. After two years gaining experience in every aspect of the kitchen, an opportunity to travel to work in India came unexpectedly. Reacting to his instinct and a sense of adventure, Will travelled half way across the world and moved to Mumbai where, over the next two years, he learnt his Indian cookery skills as Head Chef.

Winning 'Best New European Restaurant' in South Mumbai in less than a year, Will then acted as consultant to one of Mumbai's oldest and most established restaurants, before embarking on a three month journey to discover more about India's diverse cuisine.

After two years away, Will returned to the UK in 2014. Heading straight to one of London's top Indian restaurants, Will worked alongside chef Vivek Singh at Cinnamon Kitchen and learnt to refine the food and flavours of his travels. Will was inspired to set up his own modern Indian restaurant, and in 2015 an opportunity arose. Joining forces with Rik Campbell, a close friend from university, the young duo opened their first restaurant and named it Kricket; their aim to champion the rise of and redefine a new-wave approach to modern Indian food. Within a year of opening his Soho restaurant, Will was awarded national chef of the year by the Asian curry awards.

This is his first cook book.

MENU PLANS

SPRING MENU

Peanut and Pomegranate Poha, p. 35

Samphire Pakoras with Tamarind
& Date Chutney, p. 140

Cured Trout in Kasundi Mustard, p. 47

Lamb Galouti Kebab with Chutney
& Burnt Onion Raita, p. 86

Elderflower & Rhubarb Kulfi
with Sesame Brittle, p. 172

SUMMER MENU

Bhel Puri, P. 127

Oysters in Coconut Cream
with Green Chilli Granita, p. 52

Smoked Aubergine with
Sesame Raita & Papdi Gathya, p. 143

Grilled Langoustines with Pickled
Turmeric & Lasooni Butter, p. 51

Duck Breast with Sesame
& Tamarind Sauce, p. 92

Alphonso Mango Sorbet
with Chilli & Coconut, p. 171

AUTUMN MENU

Torched Mackerel with
Gooseberry Chutney, p. 44

Hyderabad Baby Aubergine
with Coconut & Curry Leaf, p. 134

Hake with Malai Sauce, p. 41

Clove Smoked Wood Pigeon
with Chanterelles & Peas, p.92

Jaggery Treacle Tart
with Milk Ice Cream, p. 161

WINTER MENU

Bonemarrow and Cep Kulcha, p. 23

Jersey Royal Aloo Chaat, p. 128

Butter Garlic Crab, p. 65

Gana's Pork Cheek Coorg, p. 90

Cardamom Kheer with Rhubarb Purée
& Carom Seed Crumble, p. 166

INDEX

Published in 2018 by Hardie Grant Books, an imprint of Hardie Grant Publishing

Hardie Grant Books (London)
5th & 6th Floors
52–54 Southwark Street
London SE1 1UN

Hardie Grant Books (Melbourne)
Building 1, 658 Church Street
Richmond, Victoria 3121

hardiegrantbooks.com

British Library Cataloguing-in-Publication Data. A catalogue record for this book is available from the British Library.

Kricket by Will Bowlby
ISBN: 978-1-78488-158-0

Publisher: Kate Pollard
Commissioning Editor: Kajal Mistry
Senior Editor: Molly Ahuja
Publishing Assistant: Eila Purvis
Art Direction, Design and Layout: Run For The Hills (runforthehills.com)
Photographer: Hugh Johnson
Photography Assistant: Dave Gatenby
Photo on pages 12–13 © Joe Woodhouse
Recipe Editor: Wendy Hobson
Proofreader: Laura Nickoll
All illustrations © Myoung Chung, except for page 83 © Lenia Hauser
Food Stylists: Laurie Perrie and Natalie Thomson
Prop Stylist: Linda Berlin
Retoucher: Butterfly Creatives
Indexer: Cathy Heath
Colour Reproduction by p2d

Printed and bound in China by 1010